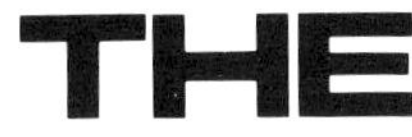

THE Bristol LH

A Pictorial Survey

All four of Eastern National LHs passed to Hedingham & District Omnibuses in 1982, and are seen here on parade at the Sible Hedingham depot, being all 'at home' for annual MOT testing in December 1983. The destination blinds display the four routes which Hedingham provide into Colchester.

G. R. Mills

ISBN 0-86093-341-1

Typesetting by:
Aquarius Typesetting Services, New Milton, Hants.

Printed in Great Britain by:
Biddles Ltd., Guildford, Surrey.

Published by:
Oxford Publishing Co.
Link House
West Street
POOLE, Dorset

The vast majority of LH chassis were built as buses, with bodies by ECW at Lowestoft, for the NBC subsidaries. Similarly, many of the shorter LHS model were also bodied in Suffolk, with the same style high quality coachwork. Lincolnshire Road Car were the pioneers of ECW buses on LHS chassis, with a batch of ten 35 seaters, numbered 1801-10. One of these, No.1807 (JVL 618H), is seen out on test by ECW staff in August 1969 passing the Lowestoft Corporation bus depot.

D. G. Savage

THE

LH

A PICTORIAL SURVEY

G. R. MILLS

Oxford Publishing Company

THE LH AS A BUS FOR ALL AREAS

MOORSIDE

Left: A West Yorkshire example No. 1178 (OWT 784M) at Kettlewell in the North Yorkshire moorland area.
D. G. Savage

SEASIDE

Right: One of United's vast LH army, No. 1692 (XUP 692R), leaves Scarborough for Whitby in July 1982.
G. R. Mills

LAKESIDE

Left: An ex-London Transport LHS, (OJD 14R) awaits mountaineers at Bowness Pier beside Lake Windermere.
J. Burnett

INTRODUCTION

Bristol finally ceased production in 1983 after 75 years of successful bus chassis production. Old half-cab double deckers and saloons have fond memories for operating staff and enthusiasts alike. More modern replacements such as the Lodekka breed (still front-engined design), and the underfloor saloons (LS and MW), were again models held in high regard. The final Bristol range included the rear-engined 'brigade' of the VR double decker and RE saloon chassis, which were eventually available to all operators, whereas previously the manufacturer's products had been restricted to the Tilling Group (Transport Holding Companies later National Bus Co.).

However, the LH (Lightweight chassis, Horizontal engine) was the first type produced by the highly-respected Bristol Commercial Vehicles for direct open market competition with the popular Bedford and Ford PSV range. The type was produced, over the 1968-83 period, in three sizes; LHS (short), LH (standard) and LHL (long), basically for 26/30/36 foot bodies respectively. The vast majority had Leyland 401 power units although early models were fitted with a 400 (Cub type), whilst a Perkins H6 was offered as an alternative.

The LH was very popular, both new and second-hand, with independent operators, as an economical and reliable vehicle. However, they were not so well-liked by company bus staff, principally because they were operating in fleets which had a majority of semi-automatic controlled gearboxes, whereas the bulk of LH chassis were manual operation. Notable exceptions were supplied to East Midland, LTE, Midland General/Mansfield District, United Counties, and an initial batch of six to Bristol Omnibus Co.

The contents of this album include a representative illustration of every major LH/LHS operator, plus a list of all those supplied new, which in turn shows an example of each make of coachwork which graced the breed; i.e. Alexander, Duple, ECW, East Lancs, Marshall, Northern Counties, Plaxtons, Weymann and Willowbrook. I apologise, in advance, to those companies whose LH/LHS/LHLs had to be left out, but to accommodate the variety of LH photographs another three volumes would have been necessary!

In this volume, it is intended to portray a cross-section of the wide ranging diversity operated in the private sector in England, Scotland, Wales and the Channel Islands. Even a non-PSV buyer is represented with a 'Van Plan' pantechnicon, whilst even vehicles prepared for export are shown. Irish visitors to the mainland are also to be found in the comprehensive coverage. No apology is made for the lack of 'gimmick' photography, popular with the trade press, but disliked by the majority of enthusiasts; i.e. vehicles obscured by bushes, bus shelters, people or hard shadows. The intention is to show clear details of bodywork, liveries and fleetnames/numbers, and not plant life, concrete constructions or shapely females; however appealling to most busmen the latter may be!

All this work would not have been possible without wide reaching help and assistance from diverse sources, and consultation of the excellent range of exhaustive fleet histories published by the PSV Circle is duly acknowledged. To the many and numerous photographers who so willingly supplied excellent prints (regrettably, not all could be accommodated); those used are duly accredited. To the vast number of operators and members of the trade who co-operated in the quest for completion, my thanks are extended. Special mention is due to M. M. Bateman and T. Lawson (Plaxtons), S. J. Brown (Leyland), D. G. J. Burch (Thamesdown), C. Carr (Bristol O. C.), B. Holden (British Caledonian), A. Macfarlane (Bristol C. V.), D. R. MacGregor (Hedingham), P. I. Newman (Ensign), C. Taylor (Reliance) and S. Taylor (Arlington). On the domestic front my thanks go to D. G. Savage, C. Shipp, and G. W. Watts who kindly checked the proofs; Pam Stewart (Colchester Telephone Area Art Club Secretary) for the superb drawings, and to my wife, Ann, for the mapwork.

Finally, grateful thanks go to T. M. Smith of Norwich (Norfolk Bluebird), who was responsible for initially getting me hooked on the 'breed' but has, up to the time of writing, still to show his ultimate faith by operating one in his own fleet!

G. R. Mills
Colchester
May 1984

After taking delivery of a batch of eight LH/ECW B45F in both 1969 and 1970, all sixteen of which were of the flat screen style body, Thames Valley never had any of the later curved screen variety. By the time the newer design batch arrived in 1975, the company's fleet had been merged with Aldershot & District and formed the fleetname Alder Valley. Three of the final batch are seen together at Bracknell in May 1980. No. 540 (KPA 351P), about to leave for the afternoon schools extras, is followed by No. 539 (KPA 350P) whilst No. 535 (KPA 346P) waits on the forecourt in this 'wall to wall' LH scene. *D. G. Savage*

Midland

Plate 1: The second Scottish Bus Group company to receive the LH model was Alexander (Midland) with two registration batches supplied in 1970. The first eight were SMS 671-8H whilst a further eleven arrived as SWG 669-79H and were numbered MLH (Midland LH) 1-19 and delivered in cream with royal blue flash and window surrounds. No. MLH 10 (SWG 670H). A Pitlochry (PY)-based coach, leaves its home town for Aberfeldy on route 144 when seen in May 1970.

D. G. Savage

Plate 2: The Scottish Bus Group examples were all fitted with Perkins H6 engines, and the Alexander Y type body. A typical example, No. MLH 12 (SWG 672H) is seen, when ten years old, awaiting the evening peak loading for a local run. The destination is displayed on the windscreen (typical SBG practice) and the vehicle is on route 95 from Falkirk bus station in September 1980 when based at Larbert (L). It sports the new style fleetname, incorporating blue flag/white cross, Scottish motif and name.

G. R. Mills

Plate 3: The last batch of eight delivered to Midland were also the last LHs supplied to the Scottish Bus Group. Registered BWG 334-41L, the first five were 41 seat coaches, as those previously placed in service, whilst the final three were 45 seat buses. One of the trio, No. MLH41 (BWG 341L) is seen in August 1977 departing from Buchanan Street bus station, Glasgow, on service back to its home base of Kirkintilloch.

D. G. Savage

EASTERN SCOTTISH

Eastern Scottish

Plates 4 5 & 6: Scottish Omnibuses Ltd. trade as Eastern Scottish and the vehicles carry the trading name in different styles of fleetname. The first LH chassis ordered by the Scottish Bus Group were eighteen, supplied in 1970 to Scottish Omnibuses Ltd. with Alexander Y type bodies, fitted with 38 coach seats and delivered in cream with green band livery, as shown by No. YA318 (OSF 318G), a Musselburgh vehicle, loading for an 8 day tour to Eastbourne at Jedburgh, the last pick up 'just north of the border' in June 1971 (*top*). The batch, OSF 315-332G, were all later demoted to stage carriage duties by reseating with 45 bus seats and repainting into reverse livery, as shown by the same vehicle (by now allocated to Scottish Omnibuses' main Airdrie depot) recoded to A318 (Y prefix indicated touring coach), seen arriving at Coatbridge bus station in July 1976 (*below*). The bus has another 15 minutes journey time left to complete the route to Clarkston on service 217 from Glasgow. The script coach-type fleetname has been replaced by the then standard bus style, not unlike the contemporary NBC style then in vogue. No.A322 (OSF 322G) (*centre*) was one of a pair repainted in the attractive blue livery of Baxter's of Airdrie, and based at Victoria, Airdrie (ex-Baxter's depot), and is seen at rest in Coatbridge in July 1976.

G. R. Mills & D. G. Savage

EX-LONDONS GO NORTH OF THE BORDER

Plate 7: London Transport advertised both their BL (LH) and BS (LHS) classes for sale direct. Grampian Regional Council's Department of Transport, at Aberdeen, took advantage of the modern units on offer by acquiring four BLs to join a small batch of Leyland National saloons and a vast number of Atlantean AN68/ Alexander double deckers. The quartet was the first Bristol/ECW combination in this most northerly municipal operator in the British Isles. No.48 (KJD 412P), smartly attired in cream and green, is seen in King Street, in July 1983.

R. J. Hefford

Plate 8: London Country had all LHS models classified BL or BN (narrow versions). Former No. BN40 (GPD 308N) was also one of four which went to tartan country. Joining the well-known Rennies of Dunfermline fleet in Fife, which for many years has always had a strong Leyland bias, they were repainted ivory with functional signwriting, plus logo. The LHS/ ECW is seen during July 1983 in company with another LCBS compatriot in the shape of an AEC Reliance/Park Royal RP class vehicle.

R. J. Hefford

Plate 9: In April 1972, the well-known World Wide Coaches of London SE5, with extensive tourist trade to Scotland, formed World Wide (Scotland) Ltd., based on the business acquired from Whitefords of Lanark. The two World Wide companies passed to Geo. Ewer (Grey-Green Coaches) N16 in April 1974, but the Scottish company was only retained until March 1978 when the Whiteford family regained control. This company now operates a very mixed fleet, which includes OJD 44R, an ex-LT bus, still in original red livery but with the Nationwide name adopted, and this vehicle is seen at rest in Quarry Garage, Lesmanagow, in July 1983, keeping company with an ex-Lothian (Edinburgh) Seddon midibus.

R. J. Hefford

SCOTLAND'S best known COACH FLEET

Plate 10: Park's of Hamilton have, in recent years, become synonymous with large batches of new Volvos. However, back in the 1970s, the intake was AEC and Bedford, plus a pair of LHL6L vehicles delivered in May 1972. These were the first LHLs to go to a Scottish operator. One of the pair is seen when only a month old, on a day trip to Troon, resplendent in unrelieved jet black livery, offset with pale blue curtains. However, both vehicles were sold a year later, but five of the LHS models purchased enjoyed a longer life with Park's.

G. R. Mills

Plate 11: BGG 155S was the only Duple version supplied to Park's. New in May 1978, it is seen in the constant traffic flow in Edinburgh's busy Princes Street, on a very wet day in August 1978. After only three months use, it has unfortunately suffered the loss of a front wheel disc and had a replacement front glass. The vehicle was sold four years later.

G. R. Mills

Plate 12: The newest of four Plaxton-bodied LHS vehicles supplied to Park's was this model, new in October 1978, seen at the famed Holyrood Palace in Edinburgh in August 1981. It is in company with one of the many and numerous foreign coaches which visit the Royal Scottish residence.

G. R. Mills

THE LHS NORTH OF THE BORDER

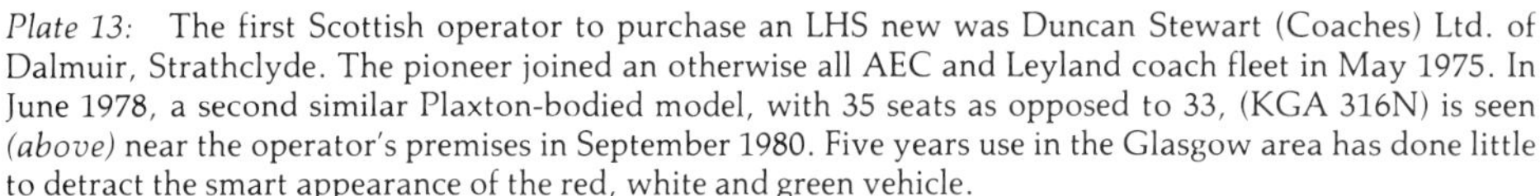

Plate 13: The first Scottish operator to purchase an LHS new was Duncan Stewart (Coaches) Ltd. of Dalmuir, Strathclyde. The pioneer joined an otherwise all AEC and Leyland coach fleet in May 1975. In June 1978, a second similar Plaxton-bodied model, with 35 seats as opposed to 33, (KGA 316N) is seen *(above)* near the operator's premises in September 1980. Five years use in the Glasgow area has done little to detract the smart appearance of the red, white and green vehicle.

G. R. Mills

Plate 14: Southern Coaches (NM) Ltd., of Barrhead, Strathclyde, owned by the Wallace family, a famed Scottish surname, have had four of the LH breed. The first, an LHL supplied in 1972 with Plaxton Elite C53F body, was really a southern coach by 1978 when acquired by the large Baker fleet in Weston-super-Mare. The second was the standard LH model, with a Plaxton Supreme C45F body, supplied in 1976. The final pair were 1978/9 LHS vehicles with Supreme-style bodies. The majority of the coaches are named in a Southern series of names carried on the back glasses; e.g. the LH was *Southern Emperor*, whilst JSU 342T, seen here, is *Southern Crest*. As the fleet is based in the same road as Ailsa Bus, nine new Volvos were taken into stock between 1977 and 1982, in the smart cream and green livery. The newest LHS is seen at the operator's Barshagra Garage, in September 1980.

G. R. Mills

Silver Fox
EDINBURGH

Plate 15: An LHL/Plaxton, (TDU 539R) was new to Deluxe, Mancetter, Warks, in April 1977, passing to Killick & Vincent (Blue Link) Dallington, E. Sussex in September 1978. It finally arrived north of the border to join the black and white Bedford fleet of Silver Fox, in March 1979. Seen in pouring rain at Pollock Halls of Residence of Edinburgh University, it awaits student transfers, in August 1979.

G. R. Mills

Plate 16: A month after the acquisition of the LHL, an LHS was acquired from Thistle, of Doncaster, who had purchased the vehicle new two years earlier. Silver Fox is the trading name of the Edinburgh & Lothian Transit Co. Ltd., and the vehicle is seen departing from the Leith premises in September 1980. The acquisition of the two Bristols was followed by two new Volvos in 1979 and a third in 1981. These were joined by a fourth heavyweight, when an ex-demonstrator DAF was acquired in 1982.

G. R. Mills

Plates 17 & 18: The hybrid Road-Rail LH, owned by the North East London Polytechnic of Dagenham, visits Scotland, It is seen parked in Canongate, part of the 'Royal Mile' from Edinburgh Castle to Holyrood Palace, on 1st September 1980, during the 34th Edinburgh International Festival week. The vehicle (NEL 847M) was ex-Hants & Dorset in November 1979 and has been kept in basic NBC poppy red with white band livery. In May 1980, it toured various towns and was equipped with photographic displays to promote public interest. By July 1980, the conversion to allow trials was completed by the Lucas Aerospace Shop Stewards' Committee in London. The test runs were made on the six mile section of the West Somerset Railway between Bishop Lydeard and Crowcombe, near Taunton, in August 1980. It subsequently made the long journey north, as shown in the above front and rear views.

G. R. Mills

The Road-Rail mechanism is shown here removed from the front end of the bus. A special feature is the use of pneumatic tyres which run on both the road and the rail. When the vehicle runs on the rails the flanged guide wheels take only a small proportion of the load and actually steer the main pneumatic tyres along the track. When the vehicle approaches a curve in the track the guide axle follows the curve and hence pushes the lever link to one side. The lever movement here is transferred via the steering links to slightly turn all of the pneumatic tyres to let the vehicle safely negotiate the curve. The hybrid system allows the vehicle to switch smoothly between road and rail using the retractable guide wheels. A second guide axle at the back of the bus ensures that the rear is held on the track. An ordinary steering mechanism guides it on the road.

A vehicle running on pneumatic tyres has the following advantages :

* Less shock is transmitted to the chassis which can thus be of lighter construction.
* As rubber has a better grip on steel rails the vehicle can climb steeper gradients.
* Standard commercial vehicle components can be used.
* Due to flexibility it enables use to be made of any existing rail or road.

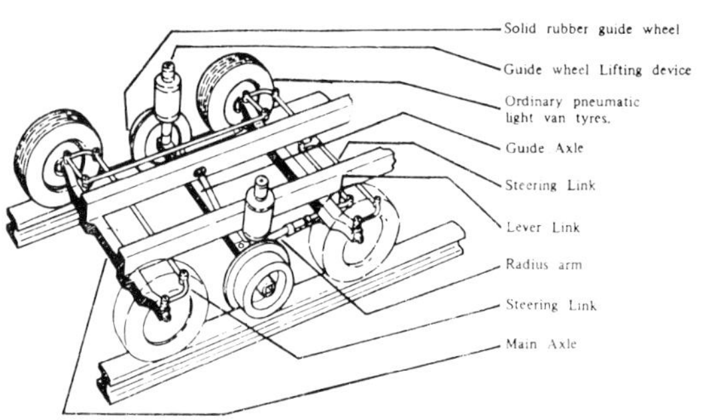

PTEs PRESENT A UNIQUE PLAXTON PURCHASE

Plate 19: Glasgow's first coach, an LHS6L with Supreme-style 35 seater body (VDS 216R), was built for G. West, Great Glen, Leics., in 1977, to replace a Bedford VAS Duple 29 seater. In the event, the vehicle, in ochre and white, was diverted to Greater Glasgow PTE. It was numbered C1 (coach one) when joined by three Leyland Panthers with Alexander W type bodies, rebuilt to coaches by the GG PTE and renumbered C2-C4. These were later reinforced by eight Leyland Leopard/Duples during 1978-1980 which became C5-C12. The coach fleet represents a very low percentage of the vast total strength of what became Strathclyde PTE.

A. Millar

Plate 20: Tyne & Wear PTE entered coaching with the purchase of two Newcastle businesses; R. Armstrong Ltd. and Galleys Coaches Ltd., in 1973. Fleet numbers 1-99 have been allotted to the coach fleet which operate from Slatyford depot and the vehicles carry Armstrong Galley fleetnames. The only LHS owned, a 35 seater new in 1977 as No. 75, is seen at Blackpool in October 1978, resplendent in yellow and cream livery.

D. G. Savage

UNITED

United Automobile Services Ltd. were prolific operators of the LH in ECW bus body form, and 200 were purchased new, whilst another small batch was acquired second-hand, initially from Alder Valley and Trent, and others were acquired later from Provincial, Southern National and Southern Vectis. Five coach versions were a more unusual order and, furthermore, two from the batch moved to Lincolnshire to become a unique pair with their second operators.

Plate 21: The first batch of LHs included ten delivered in 1968, with a mixed bag of registrations. Commencing with THN-F, three late deliveries were reregistered UHN-G, whilst the 1969 allocations commenced with YHN-H, followed by AHN-H. The AHN mark reappeared again on LH models with the 1974 deliveries, when the AHN-M series was current. No. 1514, the fourteenth LH delivered to United, pulls off Richmond Market Place, one of the largest in the country, in June 1971. Note the position of the fleetname on the waistband to allow for the advertising panel.

D. G. Savage

Plate 22: Nine ex-Alder Valley LHs, all new to Thames Valley, were acquired during 1976/7. The first four were 1971 examples which were all employed on Durham City services, as exemplified by No. 1498 (ABL 122J), seen on local duties in the city, in April 1977. The vehicle has the NBC logo and fleetname on the roof, but has retained the white band, a feature which eventually was to disappear on all repainted vehicles in later years.

D. G. Savage

CUMBERLAND

Cumberland is one of the smaller constituents of the NBC and is based on Whitehaven, with depots at Keswick, Maryport, Millom, Wigton and Workington. Only eighteen LH models have been operated by this company, seventeen of which were ECW B45F models. The 'odd man out' is illustrated below.

Plate 35: A unique vehicle in the Cumberland fleet which, for the first three sporting seasons of its life was used by Whitehaven Rugby League F. C. No. 1310 (WAO 289H), a 1970 Plaxton Elite C45F, is seen arriving at Blackpool Central, in October 1976, for the annual illuminations. Withdrawn in 1978, it saw further service with Lewingtons of Abridge, Essex, and was still regularly in service, in a white plus blue band livery, when the company went into liquidation in March 1982, after which it was regrettably sold as scrap by Ensign, the Purfleet-based dealer.

D. G. Savage

Plate 36: Representing the seventeen standard ECW B45F models, No. 108 (XRM 108J) was one of the final batch of eleven (Nos. 106-116) delivered in October 1970. It is seen in Carlisle bus station, where some of the numerous Ribble vehicles work on ex-United services inherited in 1969. This vehicle displays a short-lived fleetname style, in the lower case lettering used in a period 'twixt the Tilling underlined pattern and before the introduction of the NBC corporate image name on the roof.

D. G. Savage

Plate 37: The second LH supplied to Crosville, No. SLP145 (CFM 145G) was new in 1969 with a Perkins power unit, hence the letter P in the SLP fleet number prefix. It is seen arriving in Caernarvon on service N95 from Pwllheli in June 1976, with Rhyl local adverts on the side panel. In the background, the Clynnog & Trevor service to Pwllheli, is provided by an AEC Reliance/Beadle, previously owned by Maidstone & District.

D. G. Savage

Plate 38: This is one of the second batch of LHs, with ECW 45 seat bodies, as previous, and Perkins engines. No. SLP156 (DFM 156H) is seen in the final all green livery, on a colliery service in Wrexham, in August 1975.

G. R. Mills

Plate 39: In June 1978, the entire United Counties LH fleet was acquired by Crosville, which involved thirteen ECW saloons, all with a similar body specification to Crosville's initial batches. Mechanical variance included the Leyland 401 power unit, hence the SLL code fleet second letter L in the fleet number prefix and the semi-automatic transmission. No. SLL998 (XBD 411J) is seen at Bangor, in July 1979, heading for a typical Welsh destination!

M. A. Penn

CROSVILLE

Crosville operated sixteen LHs in 1969, with flat screen ECW B45F bodies, which were powered by Perkins engines. In contrast, forty LHs were delivered 1975/6 with the curved screen ECW B43F body (two seats lost to luggage pen) and all were fitted with Leyland engines.

Plate 40: One of the penultimate registration batch in the range MCA 611-20P, No. SLL616 (MCA 616P) has the 'Wrexham' local identity name on the roof which was introduced in November 1980, and has lost the white band during the repaint/rename process, unlike the newer example *(below)*. It is seen in the bus station of its home base, with driver waiting time before taking up position on the stand for a local service to Summerhill in July 1981.

G. R. Mills

Plate 41: One of the final batch of LHs received at Crane Wharf, Chester, in 1976, (OCA 633P), a Caernarfon vehicle during 1980, is seen in July 1981 reversing into Llanrwst depot (outstation of Llandudno Junction) after a day's work on the 'Sherpa' services around Snowdonia. The 'Gwynedd Dayrider' ticket advert on the side panel mentions independent operators Deiniolen Motors, Purple Motors, Silver Star and Whiteway, with whom an interavailability of travel exists.

G. R. Mills

SELNEC PTE

Greater Manchester Transport

Plate 42: Wigan, made famous by comedians' constant references to the mythical pier for this inland town, was not absorbed in the formation of SELNEC. Local government reorganisation in 1974 widened the scope and Wigan was engulfed by the GMPTE. At the time, six LH6L vehicles with ECW flat screen style bodies (the last produced) were on order and were originally intended to be XVU 388-93M but, in the event, were delivered as BNE 763-8N. One of the batch, No. 1322 (BNE 765N) is seen in its home town on a 600 group Wigan area service, in June 1977.

D. G. Savage

Plate 43: LUT (Lancashire United Transport) was once the largest independent bus company in Great Britain. Twenty LHs were taken into stock during 1969/70, the only ones ever bodied by Northern Counties. Fitted with 39 seats and licenced for 16 standees, the buses were delivered in red and grey livery, with the Lancashire rose transfers. No. 337 (UTD 300H), the last of the batch, backs off the stands at Bolton on a crew-operated journey to Warrington, via Leigh, in October 1972. The LH fleet numbers 318-337 were adopted by the ex-LT DMS class in 1980.

G. R. Mills

Plate 44: Control of LUT passed to GMPTE around 1976 and the sunglow orange livery was gradually introduced in various forms. The LHs received an all-over application, exemplified by UTD 285H, seen in September 1980 soon after acquisition by Hewlett & Sutton, Lonsdale Coaches, Morecambe, Lancashire, owners of two examples. Despite the ambitious destination display, the pair were used largely for the conveyance of workers to the large power-station at Heysham; a duty which keeps many of the sulphur yellow contract fleet constantly busy.

G. R. Mills

UNITED

Plate 29: Numerous United Automobile vehicles, working wholly within or marginally cross-boundary services in the Tyne & Wear area, carry the PTE yellow and white livery. Three LH buses were so treated, as shown by No. 1681 (NGR 681P), one of a pair active from Whitley Bay depot when this April 1984 view was taken in Newcastle's Haymarket bus station. Note the Tyne & Wear Transport transfers on the vehicle and the PTE's Travel Centre fascia in the background.

D. G. Savage

Plate 30: The North is synonymous with cold bleak winters, and 1983/84 lived up to tradition with generous snowfalls in United's operating area. The effects were still in evidence in this chill March 1984 shot, in stark winter sunlight at Morpeth bus station. No. 1721 (VDV 125S), new in 1977 as a Western National vehicle, was a Southern National bus based at Yeovil prior to its transfer northwards. Attractively repainted in dual-purpose white and red livery, the vehicle was fitted with 37 coach seats by United Automobile Services. The destination is in keeping with the a southern dwellers' concept of the 'frozen' north!

G. Stainthorpe

Plate 31: The registration of this LH (WAE) could well be taken to mean 'Wander Across England', as the bus has had four NBC owners in six short years of life. New to the Bristol O. C. as No. 440, it passed with numerous shed-mates to Hants & Dorset as No. 3835. It escaped the Hampshire Bus/Wilts & Dorset set-up by transfer to Provincial as No. 87. WAE 192T is seen as United No. 1723 in this April 1984 view, as it prepares to leave the new bus station in Durham. With many more years life ahead, it is a matter of some speculation how many more homes it is destined to have.

D. G. Savage

LH AS AN NBC COACH

Plate 32: Whilst the majority of the NBC subsidiaries bought the LH chassis, few had coach bodies fitted. The largest batch with Plaxton Elite coachwork was five 41 seaters delivered during 1970, in cream livery with a broad green band (Tyne, Tees, and Thames style) to United Automobile Services, exemplified by No. 1082 (BHN 982H) at rest, in July 1970, at Inverness on a Highlands tour.

T. W. W. Knowles

Plate 33: Nos. 1081-5 (BHN 981-5H), under the NBC corporate image, became just another batch of white Plaxton coaches. The National Express network took the United coaches to even more distant and unfamiliar places. No. 1084 (BHN 984H) is seen awaiting refuelling at the Kelvedon depot (Essex) of National Travel (South East) having worked service 352 down from Sunderland to Colchester. The 11 hour journey incorporated calls at Darlington, Leeds, Doncaster, Peterborough, Cambridge and Ipswich.

D. G. Savage

Plate 34: BHN 981/2H passed to Lincolnshire Road Car in 1979 and remained on long express routes at peak times as shown by BHN 981H, as 1601, at Battersea Wharf (NBC's London parking area), in July 1981. The neat coach has worked express service 467 from Mablethorpe and Skegness, via Peterborough, into Victoria Coach Station, and prepares to work a 468 service back to its home depot of Grimsby.

D. G. Savage

SMALL ONES OF MANCHESTER

Plate 45: Two LHS models were delivered to the Greater Manchester PTE in 1975. Although the SELNEC (South East Lancashire, North-East Cheshire) PTE formed in October 1969, had been replaced by GMPTE in April 1974, the name SELNEC Travel lingered on for a limited period on the coach fleet. JND 992N, seen when very new in May 1975, approaches the coach division garage in Charles Street, Stockport.

G. R. Mills

Plate 46: The twin brother to the LHS illustrated above, JND 993N, is seen in Eccleston Place, Victoria, awaiting its turn for a wash and refuel at Samuelsons garage in December 1978. It wears the final livery of white with brown and orange stripes and the 'Charterplan' fleetname and M symbol adopted by GMPTE, which replaced the simpler white and orange scheme. A third LHS, also with the 'diddy' Duple Dominant I body, was supplied to GMPTE in 1976.

G. R. Mills

Plate 47: In February 1982, JND 993N took up residence in the Dorset resort of Weymouth, being purchased by Bluebird Coaches Ltd. It is seen, in June 1983, at the company's garage premises repainted into duo blue and white. In the background stands a second LHS coach, but with a Plaxton Supreme body. New in 1978 to the British Council, London, as UYY 198S, the latter was purchased by Bluebird in August 1980.

G. R. Mills

TWO Rs IN LANCASHIRE?

Plate 48: Rossendale Borough Council was formed in April 1974 from the neighbouring fleets of both Rawtenstall C. T. and Haslingden C. T. The maroon and cream livery of the latter was initially adopted, but this evolved into the present crimson lake and cream scheme as worn by the LHS *(left)*. No. 51 (SND 551X) is one of a pair with rare East Lancashire 28 seat bodies, the only two LHS chassis so fitted, new in 1982 and the first of the LH breed to be operated by the Borough. No. 51 is seen in Rawtenstall bus station, in September 1982, with the then newly-adopted green logo, representing the Rossendale Hills, on the side panels.

A. J. Kennedy

Plate 49: The green Rossendale Hills logo is further illustrated on TPJ 56S, the ex-London Country LHS which was added to the small fleet, seen in Rossendale depot at Rawtenstall in August 1983.

T. W. W. Knowles

Plate 50: Ribble Motor Services have been staunch Leyland customers since 1923. It is thus the non-standard purchases, i.e. with chassis built beyond Lancashire, that have usually aroused most interest. Small batches of saloons have usually been the monopoly busters, e.g. Dennis Aces in the 1930s, Sentinels in the 1950s, and Bedford coaches in the 1960s. In 1980, a pair of LHS vehicles with familiar ECW bodies, were delivered for the Ribble Valley midibus services based on Clitheroe. Regularly driven by a lady driver, the services have been publicised as 'Betty's Bus' as shown by No. 271 (FBV 271W) on the Lancashire Moors in May 1982.

M. Fowler

MUNICIPAL MIDIS

Plate 51: Preston, Lancs., with its extremely close location to Leyland, was always a stronghold of locally-produced chassis. The requirement for a small bus was met by three Leyland-engined LHS vehicles with Duple Dominant coach bodies. Two were fitted with bus seating, as illustrated by No. 343 (PHG 243P) seen backing off the stands in Preston bus station.

D. G. Savage

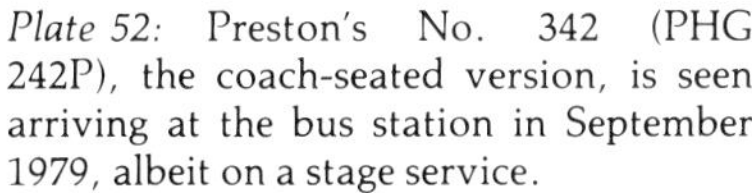

Plate 52: Preston's No. 342 (PHG 242P), the coach-seated version, is seen arriving at the bus station in September 1979, albeit on a stage service.

G. R. Mills

Plate 53: Two LHS/ECW (30 coach seats) vehicles for a special cross-town facility launched as 'Stagecoach Service' with a special headboard carried in the brackets below the front grille, were bought by Northampton Transport. KBD 21V and KBD 22V were new in October 1979. The latter is seen at picturesque Dallington Green in May 1980. The boards have since been removed revealing a large fleet number beneath.

G. R. Mills

LOVELY LITTLE MOVERS

WEST YORKSHIRE PTE → MERSEYSIDE and TAYSIDE

JUG 352 – 7N

Plate 54: Of the six little LHS models which once ran around Leeds, three went to Liverpool, and three went to Dundee. New in July 1975 to the West Yorkshire PTE, and carrying 'Metro' fleetnames, they were basically for car-park/shopping services and occasional private-hire work. No. 39 (JUG 355N) is seen in May 1976 approaching Leeds Central bus station.

D. G. Savage

Plate 55: The first of the batch of six went to Merseyside PTE in 1980 to work the Toxteth Community Service. The ECW body had retained the verona green as a base colour with increased coverage, plus dark brown window uprights and skirt. No. 2156 (JUG 352N) is seen in Elliot Street, Liverpool, in March 1983. The advert amidships reads 'The Link-Up' Toxteth's own midibus, with a drawing of an LH as the centrepiece.

D. G. Savage

Plate 56: The three of the batch that ventured north of the border arrived in Dundee too late to receive the old green livery, but received the Tayside duo blue to the same layout as they had originally been painted in Metro service. No. 225 (JUG 356N) one of a pair working normal PSV services, is seen waiting time in the town centre, in August 1980. The third member was allocated to the Planning Department.

G. R. Mills

WEST YORKSHIRE

Plate 57: AWR 887G as No. LH19 (later No. 1169) pictured in red with cream window surrounds, and with fleetnames mid-way on the side panels, negotiates the narrow streets of Kettlewell in June 1971. The vehicle has a picturesque journey to Skipton to complete, from the North Riding, passing Conistone Moor, following the course of the River Wharfe, the Wharfedale area of the Pennines.

D. G. Savage

Plate 58: Also part of the 1969 intake of twenty six LH/ECW B45F vehicles with a vast range of registration marks, was No. 1156 (originally No. LH6) YWW 540G which is seen in NBC livery in April 1975 when a Harrogate vehicle, although based at Pateley Bridge sub-depot. Had the vehicle survived, the cream band would have disappeared on its next repaint.

D. G. Savage

EAST MIDLAND

East Midland vehicles once sported a distinctive livery of chrome yellow with chocolate bands, which was discontinued after 1956, on the adoption of spray painting, in favour of a mundane deep red, with cream round the window frames.

Plate 59: East Midland's first batch of LHs arrived thirteen years too late to see the old livery. No. O525 (UNN 525G) was one of ten delivered in 1969 with Willowbrook 45 seat bodies, and is seen departing Doncaster Waterdale bus station. Withdrawal of the batch began in December 1979 and all were withdrawn by December 1980. Before their final demise, some of this unique set of buses, the only LHs bodied by Willowbrook, were hired to Hulleys of Baslow, Derbyshire, during a period of acute vehicle difficulties, further aggravated by severe weather conditions.

D. G. Savage

Plate 60: Eight years passed before East Midland took delivery of any further LH vehicles. The vehicles materialised as SNU 851-3R, built concurrently with SNU 384-7R supplied to Trent. All seven have 43 seat ECW bodies as illustrated by No. 853, in green livery, seen at Tickhill, and bound for Doncaster in July 1982, in the days before the all over green livery gained an unfortunate grip on the NBC's paint style.

G. R. Mills

MIDLAND GENERAL PASS TO TRENT

Plate 61: Midland General's first batch of LHs was delivered in 1969 in distinctive cream livery, with black window surrounds, as shown by No. 115 (BNU 677G), one of six identical vehicles (Nos. 111-116). The bus has the joint fleetnames of Mansfield District and Midland General, but following the reorganisation split in October 1976, it passed into Trent control. It is seen in Nottingham, during the rebuilding of Mount Street bus station, in May 1969, with a blue 1958 Bristol LD6G, No. 471 (20 DRB), bound for Ripley.

G. R. Mills

Plate 62: The same bus (now under new ownership) with the new fleetname, fleet number and livery. BNU 677G, as Trent No. 405, in the NBC poppy red livery, arrives in Nottingham (King Street) having worked into the city on a hot day in July 1980. Trent had not purchased any LHs new, prior to the Midland General acquisitions. Four arrived in April 1977 followed by two diverted from Crosville the following month. Thus, with the fourteen from Midland General, Trent had a total of twenty in operation within nine months, from a previous total of nil.

D. G. Savage.

TRENT BRISTOL MUST TRAVEL

Plate 63: PNU 388R was born into fame, as it was selected as a Commercial Motor Show exhibit at Earls Court, when new, in September 1976. One of a pair delivered to Trent, both were allocated to the former North Western Road Car Co. depot at Matlock. No. 388 is seen in February 1980, still in Trent ownership but carrying East Kent fleetnames, as it was loaned from September 1979 for a special community service to William Harvey Hospital worked by Ashford depot, until replaced by a Ford A series in a unique livery. The vehicle had its Trent roof fleetname replaced prior to return to Derbyshire in March 1980.

G. R. Mills

Plate 64: The pair of vehicles mentioned above, were separated again after sale, and the twin went to United, and was based at Darlington depot, whilst PNU 388R found a new home in South Wales. It is smartly turned out with a black roof and green window surrounds, in the ownership of the Howardian High School, Cardiff, as seen in September 1982.

G. R. Mills

LINCOLNSHIRE

Although serving the City of Lincoln, the industrial Scunthorpe, the port of Grimsby, the seaside at Skegness, and small towns such as Boston, Grantham and Newark, the vast majority of the company operating area of Lincolnshire Road Car is decidedly rural. For this latter task, over 100 Bristol SC4LK models were taken into stock from 1956-61. The introduction of the LH was similarly well received with 96 being delivered from 1968-79, which resulted in the ousting of the last of the SCs in 1976.

IN THE CAPITAL

Plates 65 & 66: The first batch of LHs delivered were GVL 907-12F which entered service in July 1968. Supplied in cream livery with Tilling green window surrounds and waistband, they were fitted with 41 semi-luxury seats, suitable for 'limited stop' workings. Powered by a Perkins H6 engine, No. 1653 (GVL 909F) has made the long journey from Lincoln when seen at London's Victoria Coach Station in August 1969 *(top picture)*, after unloading the incoming passengers, in company with a Leyland Leopard/Plaxton Panorama I, an MCW Castillian of Southdown and an East Kent AEC Reliance/Park Royal. By July 1974, when the lower view was taken of the same vehicle, the livery had been revised to NBC leaf green and white, but the location is very close to the upper view, literally just around the corner in Eccleston Place, and No. 1653 waits to turn into the ex-Samuelsons garage for a refill, plus an oil/water check, before a relief working on the express service to Lincoln.

G. R. Mills

LHS IN LINCOLNSHIRE'S FLEET

Plate 67: The first production LHS models were a pair delivered to Lincolnshire Road Car Co. in late 1968. The third one of the trio, GVL 913-5G, delivered in February 1969, is seen five months later in the 'as supplied' condition, apart from a little damage repair to the front nearside corner! To the rear of the vehicle is the bus station, and away in the distance, the open door is a personnel entrance into the workshops of the Lincolnshire Road Car Company's Scunthorpe complex.

G. R. Mills

Plate 68: A further seven LHS models were delivered later in 1969. Four received G suffix registrations, whilst the final trio were JVL 927-9H. No. 1809 (JVL 928H) was chosen for special duties as the Bassetlaw Community Bus, a contract formerly provided by Leon, Finningley, with a Ford A0609. Refitted with 20 coach seats and an invalid lift, it is seen at the East Midland Retford garage in July 1979, attired in special blue, white and green livery; a striking format.

G. R. Mills

Plate 69: This is the final livery for the ultimate LHS, that lingered long enough to receive another version of NBC livery, all over unrelieved leaf green, as displayed by No. 1810 (JVL 929H) seen in Scunthorpe bus station. Proof that North Lincolnshire has an affinity with County Durham can be judged by the Binns store sign on the shopping precinct in the background.

D. G. Savage

LINCOLNSHIRE IN VARIOUS HUES

Plate 70: Lincolnshire's first batch of LHs with the restyled ECW bus body (i.e. two piece curved windscreens and curved front apron) were supplied as cream and green coaches. No. 1672 (NFE 647J) is one of six delivered in 1971 with 41 seats suitable for express services. Caught at rest in Bishops Road bus station, Peterborough, in August 1971, it is seen amongst a gaggle of Eastern Counties Lodekkas, as it takes a refreshment stop on the journey from London Victoria Coach Station.

G. R. Mills

Plate 71: On repaint, the batch lost their coach livery in favour of the NBC dual-purpose (local coach) scheme of leaf green below the windows, and white (top half), but retained the 41 semi-luxury seats. No. 1674 (NFE 649J) finally lost all express status in August 1978 when fitted with 43 bus seats. However, it was to have a final claim to fame when the lower panels were repainted brown to mark the 50th anniversary of the company. It is seen at Lincoln, in July 1980, complete with 'period' fleetname on the side panels.

D. G. Savage

Plate 72: The final batch of LHs supplied new to the company comprised nine standard buses in NBC green livery, with 43 bus seats in light ochre mock leatherette (PVC) covering, as opposed to most early batches which had the Tilling moquette. No. 1071 (DTL 547T), the penultimate Lincolnshire, delivered in 1979, is seen leaving Nottingham in July 1980 for its home base at Grantham.

D. G. Savage

SOUTH MIDLAND CHANGE OWNERS

Plate 73: The first LH of the first batch of four, supplied to Thames Valley for the South Midland coach fleet, was RJB 428F, fitted with Duple Commander III 41 seat body. This vehicle, and eleven similar coaches, passed to City of Oxford Motor Services in January 1971. The 1968 coach is seen in its final NBC white form at Cowley Road garage, Oxford, (Head Office and Works), in January 1975 as No. 28.

G. R. Mills

Plate 74: One enthusiastic buyer of this rare combination was Harris Coaches (Pengam) Ltd., based at Fleur-de-Lis, Gwent, in South Wales. In addition to a Plaxton Elite-bodied LHL, three ex-South Midland Duple Commander LHs have been operated by them. UMO 690G is seen returning to base after a morning school contract in June 1980, in the new owner's rich cream with red bands modern style livery.

G. R. Mills

Plate 75: Early in the year following the transfer of the South Midland coaches from Thames Valley to City of Oxford Motor Services, one of the last batch of LH/Duples was suitably adorned with holiday advertisements, and toured the company's area as a smart promotional exercise. No. 36 (YBL 925H) is seen outside the canteen building on its return to base at Cowley Road depot/works in Oxford on rather damp day in May 1972. Each batch, RJB 428-31F, UMO 688-91G and YBL 925-8H, all had a different front grille treatment.

G. R. Mills

UNITED COUNTIES

Although operating in some rural parts of Bedfordshire, Bucks., Cambs., Herts. and Northants, United Counties only purchased thirteen LHs for working the sparsely-populated routes. In the event, the newest ones did not survive for even eight years before their sale to Crosville, when the entire breed was sold in June 1978. However, small capacity buses have never enjoyed longevity with United Counties. For example, the Bristol SCs were sold to Red & White, Chepstow, after only seven years, whilst the SU models were expelled after a mere six years. United Counties Omnibus Co., in company with Mansfield District/Midland General, specified four speed semi-automatic transmission for all their deliveries of LH chassis.

Plates 76 & 77: SRP 401G *(above)*, new in June 1969 and one of the initial pair delivered to United Counties, was also amongst the last of the older style with shallow front screen ECW bodies. It is still in original form when seen departing from Kettering bus station, in August 1970. The lack of destination display for route 408 does not seem to have detracted the number of passengers! In November 1976, the front end was rebuilt, as per later batches portrayed by XBD 411J *(below)*, the penultimate UCOC model seen awaiting collection at the ECW works in Eastern Way, Lowestoft, in October 1970.

G. R. Mills

LUTON LITTLE 'UNS UNLOVED

In December 1969, Luton Corporation Transport took delivery of five LHS6P vehicles with ECW 37 seat bodies as Nos. 131-5 (XXE 131-5H). Staffing problems were rife and the buses were never operated. The services and vehicles passed to United Counties in January 1970, but again the five were not used. All passed to Eastern Counties in February 1970 and were re-registered WNG 101-5H. New vehicles with three owners in three months must constitute a record!

Plate 78: XXE 134H as Luton Corporation Transport No. 134, is seen in December 1969 at Kingsway depot. This vehicle became Eastern Counties WNG 104H and was initially allocated to Cambridge.

G. R. Mills

Plate 79: Eastern Counties vehicle (WNG 105H) originally XXE 135H was sent to Peterborough (PBO) depot, a town which accommodates the Perkins engine manufacturing factories, hence all the Peterborough allocation had the four circle Perkins' trademark badges on the radiator grilles. Others of the batch were scattered to such outstations as Saxmundham, Stowmarket and Thetford in their early Eastern Counties days.

G. R. Mills

Plate 80: In August 1978, WNG 105H was launched on to a new line of duty. It was reseated with 35 coach seats and repainted red and white (NBC local coach livery; i.e. dual-purpose) for the St. Ives 'Pick me up' set of routes, which included serving Huntingdon Station. Replacing an unreliable Ford A series midibus, the LHS is seen at Cambridge, in October 1979, where the routine maintenance was performed on No. LHS936, as it had become, at Hills Road depot.

G. R. Mills

SHORT COACH WITH LONG HISTORY

Plate 81: Destined to be an 'odd man out' throughout its PSV career, THX 618M was new in 1973 to Timpsons, Catford, as part of a block of six consecutive registrations. The remaining five were Duple-bodied AEC Reliances. All passed to National Travel (South East) on its formation in August 1974. The vehicle is seen at Watford Gap services area, on the M1 motorway, in June 1974, with original fleetnames.

G. R. Mills

Plate 82: Although Southern Vectis had LHS chassis with both Marshall and ECW bus bodies, THX 618M started a new fleet number series when it arrived on the island early in 1978. Smartly attired in the dual-purpose livery of leaf green and white, with blue coach seating, it became No. DP1. The neat vehicle, seen at Newport, in the lay-over bays in September 1978, has suffered some minor accident damage on the narrow road system.

G. R. Mills

Plate 83: During its stay with Southern Vectis, the destination box was rebuilt to incorporate a triple number track. This was all promptly blanked out when the 'special' was acquired by British Caledonian in March 1983. Repainted in its third livery in ten years, the attractive gold, blue and white, the vehicle is shown whilst at Gatwick maintenance area a year later. THX 618M is seen during preparation for a PSV/MOT test, as a newly delivered Airbus 310 comes in to land on a routine domestic flight.

G. R. Mills

LONDON COUNTRY SERVE THE OLD AND THE NEW

Plate 84: No. BN34 (GPD 302N) is seen passing St. Peter's Church in St. Albans, in April 1981. This town is well-known for its historical Roman associations, when it was named Verulamium, the remains of which include an amphitheatre visited by numerous school parties during the summer term. The popular BBC 'Grange Hill' school series gave extensive coverage of the principal education features during a 1983 screening. St. Albans garage was a pioneer operator of the London Country Bus Service LH, which entered service in October 1973.

G. R. Mills

Plate 85: No. BN50 (GPD 318N), by direct contrast, is seen in Stevenage New Town, in February 1976, awaiting return to its home base of Hertford, a depot which had seven of the type on regular scheduled service at the time. During the same period, Harlow, another new town, only ten miles from Hertford, had three LHs in regular use on rural routes.

G. R. Mills

LONDON COUNTRY
FINAL BATCH OF LHs

Fourteen LHS versions with 7ft. 6in. wide ECW bodies (Class BN), which were new late in 1977.

Plate 86: No. BN55, seen on a very misty day in December 1978, with both side and fog lights in use, picks up in Much Hadham, Herts. en route for the county town. The vehicle is in the original 'as supplied' livery of NBC leaf green with a white band. In 1983, with three others of the same batch, it passed to South Yorkshire PTE for 'City Nipper' work *(see below).*

G. R. Mills

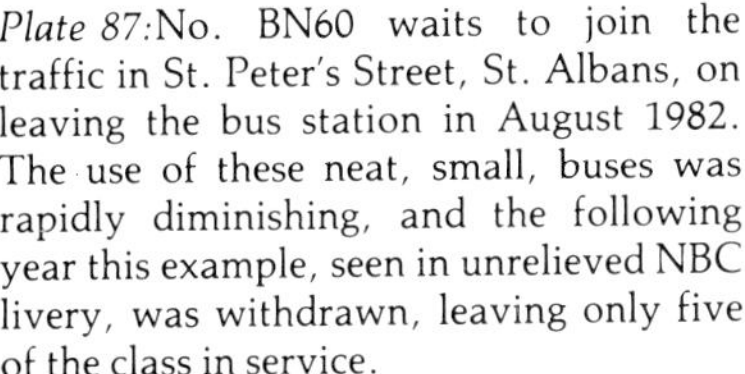

Plate 87: No. BN60 waits to join the traffic in St. Peter's Street, St. Albans, on leaving the bus station in August 1982. The use of these neat, small, buses was rapidly diminishing, and the following year this example, seen in unrelieved NBC livery, was withdrawn, leaving only five of the class in service.

G. R. Mills

Plate 88: Former No. BN65 is seen in its new livery and ownership. This is one of four which passed to the South Yorkshire PTE in February 1983 for special 'City Nipper' work in Sheffield; a group of services operating from the city centre to large housing estates. TPJ 65S, in smart tan and cream livery, is seen amongst other South Yorkshire PTE buses on display at the Sandtoft Gathering annual open day, at the Yorkshire trolley bus museum, on a very wet day in July 1983.

G. R. Mills

ODDS ON FAVOURITES FROM LONDON TRANSPORT

During 1975/6, a batch of six, followed by a further eleven LHS6L versions, with standard profile ECW 26 seat bodies, measuring 24ft. x 7ft. 6in., were delivered. Many were to replace Ford Transits on routes where the minibuses had proved inadequate.

Plate 89: No. BS7 is pictured smartly repainted in an eye-catching yellow and black livery, and is one of a pair owned by Frank Thorpe of London. The vehicle is seen at Woburn Abbey, surrounded by modern luxury coachwork entries in the annual 'Showbus' event in September 1983.

G. R. Mills

Plate 90: No. BS9, smartly turned out by London Transport for the Shillibeer 150 Year Celebrations, is seen on parade in Battersea Park Gardens in April 1979. These neat vehicles, with semi-automatic gearboxes, were eagerly sought after on resale. This bus was one of a pair acquired by Weardale Motor Services of Frosterley, Co. Durham, in 1981.

G. R. Mills

Plate 91: No. BS11 is seen, after final withdrawal by London Transport, at rest in Ensign, dealers, Purfleet premises in October 1981, prior to a mechanical check and a long journey north. The subsequent owner of this vehicle was J. Keenan & Sons, Coalhall, Drongan, who repainted it in a striking livery incorporating a series of dotted arrowheads.

G. R. Mills

ODDS ON . . . II
EX-LONDON TRANSPORT

Plate 92: No. BS13 appeared at one stage to be dogged by an unlucky stigma. Whilst parked at Ensign's yard at Purfleet, it was unfortunately so near the steam cleaner that the liquified dirt off the underside of dozens of DMS double decks was deposited on its bodywork! Suitably cleaned and repainted in grey primer, it is seen, in March 1983, prior to delivery to British Caledonian at Gatwick.

G. R. Mills

Plate 93: Transformed by a new livery of white, blue and gold, the house colours of the efficient British Caledonian Airways, OJD 13R is seen at work, at Gatwick, a year later. Four LHS vehicles and numerous Ford Transits act as crew buses, conveying the flight staff between the administration buildings and the aircraft. Ex-No. BS13 sets out with a pleasant group of tartan clad cabin 'belles' to work some p.m. flights.

G. R. Mills

Plate 94: No. BS17 was prepared for WNS Travel Ltd., 'Arrow' of Coldwaltham, in West Sussex, as shown in this September 1982 photograph at the Ensign, Purfleet premises. The yellow and white hue was short-lived as the vehicle was resold to the Mobil Oil Company of Coryton, Essex. Similarly employed as the British Caledonian examples, the bus is ideal for staff transport in the vast refinery complex beside the Thames Estuary.

G. R. Mills

LONDON TRANSPORT LOCAL LIVERIES

Plates 95 & 96: In the 1950s, the largest new batch of saloons in the London Transport Central Area fleet was the AEC Regal IV, RF class buses, operating in a staid red livery as, indeed, were the pre-war supporting cast of AEC models. In the 1960s, the AEC Swift, dubbed 'Merlins' by London Transport, appeared in various forms as Class MB, MBA and MBS. The MBA variant, a Merlin Bus Arrow, was the pioneer of route marketing by eye-catching livery variants with bold lettering, but still retained the traditional red as a basic colour. The final three of the 95 Bristol LH6Ls, with 7ft. 6in. wide ECW bodies to the normal 30ft. length, were allocated to the London Borough of Hillingdon's new service 128 in September 1977. Worked from Uxbridge garage, the initial variation to livery was the white area around the window frames being replaced by yellow, as shown on No. BL95 departing Thorpe Leisure Park in September 1980 *(above)*. Three years later the same vehicle, seen arriving at Woburn Abbey, displays an even bolder application of yellow livery *(below)*.

G. R. Mills

TOWNIES MOVE OUT INTO THE COUNTRY

EX-LONDON TRANSPORT LHs in HERTFORDSHIRE

Plate 97: KJD 438P, (one time London Transport No. BL38) was initially purchased by Smiths of Buntingford for mechanical spares for an LHS/Plaxton coach (new to Bebb, Llantwit Fadre), but the ECW body was in such good condition that it was decided to recertify the vehicle for further service. It is pictured, in February 1984, at the new owner's yard, soon after re-entry into PSV work with a 'home-made' front grille, and is sporting a Leyland badge. The LH replaced a Bedford VAS/Marshall (ex-Essex Police) on stage and school services in the Hitchin area.

G. R. Mills

Plate 98: OJD 54R (former London Transport No. BL54) was the first Bristol in the smart Sworders of Walkern fleet, joining a rare Seddon Pennine VII (Gardner 180), several Volvos, and a Van Hool Acron in coaches; plus Leyland Leopard and Bedford YRT buses. The LH is seen, in December 1983, with immaculate brown and grey paintwork, at the operator's premises from where it is used on school contracts in Stevenage. The LH found great favour with the owners, and was joined by an ex-Bristol Omnibus Co. vehicle a few months later, with similar ECW body but with a manual gearbox.

G. R. Mills

LONDON COUNTRY
LHs LEAVE HOME

Part of the first eleven (RPH 101-111L) delivered in 1973 as Nos. BL1-11.

Plate 99: FOR SALE — In the silvan setting of the car-park of British Aerospace at Weybridge, Surrey, in April 1983, on the occasion of the annual open day at the London Bus Preservation Group museum at Cobham, London Country's first LH, No. BL1 (RPH 101L), proclaims its availability

G. R. Mills

Plate 100: SOLD – No. BL4 has travelled many miles from its original habitat to the delightful operating area of Tally Ho! Coaches Ltd., with bases at Ivybridge and Kingsbridge. RPH 104L is seen at Kingsbridge, in May 1982, repainted into the then standard ivory with blue layer livery. The destination blind displays the quaintly vague stage service; information which, no doubt, is meaningful to the regulars in this area of South Devon, where Tally Ho! introduced a service to Salcombe in competition with Western National route 93, from April 1981.

G. R. Mills

Plate 101: IN TRAINING – No. BL6 was one of four of the class which were demoted to the driving school. The principal exterior change, apart from the obvious L plates, is the yellow band. Although the vehicle has an MA (Amersham) stencilled garage code, it is seen at Harlow (HA) depot forecourt in April 1981.

G. R. Mills

EASTERN NATIONAL

Only four LHs were ever delivered to Eastern National. Some had been allocated in previous NBC orders, but these were diverted to Bristol Omnibus Co., in exchange for a lesser number of Leyland National vehicles. The four were delivered in July 1977 concurrently with three Bristol VRs.

Plate 102: All four were initially allocated to Colchester (CR), and spent virtually their entire working careers in and out of Colchester bus station, even when on temporary loan to other depots. In August 1980, No. 1102 (UVX 6S) works a well-laden afternoon journey to a small village. The vehicle wears the final all green livery worn in company service (i.e. minus the white central band contained in the original layout).

G. R. Mills

Plate 103: In 1982, all four were withdrawn by Eastern National, after a rail strike had temporarily prolonged their stay. In October of the same year, all four re-entered service with Hedingham & District Omnibuses of Sible Hedingham, smartly repainted in duo red and cream. No. L114 (UVX 7S) moves off from the same stand on the same service, albeit a lunch time short working, as its fellow member of the quartet in *Plate 102*, but in July, four years later. The LHs were the first of this model in the Hedingham fleet, which had previously comprised a majority shareholding of Bedford Y series models for both service saloons and coaches.

G. R. Mills

HEDINGHAM & DISTRICT

ON DEMONSTRATION IN/WITH EASTERN COUNTIES

Plates 104 & 105: NHU 100F, the prototype LH, chassis No. 001, was new in February 1968 and is seen, on 29th August 1968, when only six months old, at Marks Tey roundabout on the A12 trunk road *(top)* bound for Wilder (Golden Miller) Feltham, where it was used on their 602 service to Hanworth. Whilst on demonstration, it was in Tilling green livery, until late 1969 when the touring ended, and in January 1970 it reappeared in Eastern Counties red and cream livery. In the lower picture, it is seen a month later, at Surrey Street bus station, in Norwich. In 1974 it was repainted, yet again, into the NBC poppy red and white livery, and survived ten years of company service, initially as No. LH719 and after 1977 as No. LH703.

G. R. Mills

EASTERN COUNTIES FIRST AND LAST

A ten year span from RAH 685F in 1968 to WEX 931S in 1978.

Plate 106: RAH 685F was, numerically, the first Eastern Counties LH. One of seven delivered in June 1968, it is seen in Surrey Street bus station, Norwich, in May 1969, about to work the lengthy service 14 to Ipswich, via Eye. The bus, No. LH685 is in the 'as supplied' livery of Tilling red and cream, with black lining on the mouldings between the colours, a practise discontinued on repaints. The vehicle is also displaying the vague 'service' on the destination blind; a regular occurrence which resulted in the company receiving much criticism from both press and public.

G. R. Mills

Plate 107: WEX 931S had the doubtful distinction of being the ultimate LH supplied to Eastern Counties. It was one of a pair delivered in March 1978 in poppy red with a white band, which was reduced to 'all over' red in January 1980. The vehicle, No. LH931, is seen on British Rail land, being used as an overflow parking compound for the Hills Road depot, Cambridge, in February 1982, and damage to the front fibreglass panels of the vehicle is evident.

G. R. Mills

SHOW OFFS

Plate 108: RAH 692F, new to Eastern Counties in July 1968, achieved a short claim to fame when it was exhibited at the Commercial Motor Show at Earls Court. It is seen here, in February 1970, on a local service working out of Peterborough. It served the company for a further ten years before being withdrawn and sold for scrap.

G. R. Mills

Plate 109: It was appropriate that Eastern Counties Omnibus Co. should represent ECW at a National Transport Exhibition, in view of the early history when operator and coachbuilder were very closely associated. HAH 537L was Eastern Counties' first vehicle in poppy red, whilst it was also the company's last Perkins-engined LH model. No. LH537 shares Stand 37 at Earls Court with a Southern Vectis Bristol VRT (XDL 377L) in September 1972.

W. R. Rowley

Plate 110: Fortunately the staff at the Peterborough depot of Eastern Counties recognised the rarity value of No. LH537 and brought it to a bus rally at King's Lynn in September 1980. It is pictured still fitted with the show seats (i.e. the National double N pattern), but with the exterior smartly repainted to include a white band, which it first received in 1975. No. LH537 (HAH 537L) sets off home to Peterborough depot after the day's events.

G. R. Mills

ALL CHANGE ON EASTERN COUNTIES

Plates 111 & 112: The penultimate LH delivered to Eastern Counties was No. LH930 (WEX 930S), which was supplied as a standard 43 seater service bus in March 1978. In the upper view, it is seen on normal stage duties in St. Andrews Street, Cambridge, in February 1982. The bus shelter sign quotes route 180 and 181 for the rail station, whilst a board at high level invites pedestrians to walk through a shopping precinct to Drummer Street bus station (for rival express services?). Withdrawn in September 1982 and reseated with 34 coach seats from redundant REs, whilst the back row remained original, the vehicle reappeared in February 1983 in a striking white with red band, as shown in the lower view, and is seen departing Norwich bus station in February 1984 for its home depot. The vehicle initially worked the commuter express duty from Holt each Monday to Friday, resting at Cromer every weekend.

G. R. Mills & D. G. Savage

TAYLOR MANY BRISTOLS

The old established coach operating business of Chas. Taylor, t/a Reliance Coaches, and based at Meppershall, near Shefford, Beds., has owned more LH models than any other private company in East Anglia. Altogether, thirty LHs have been operated, all in the unusual duo pink livery, and all but five were supplied new.

Plate 113: LARGE – LTM 971G was the pioneer of the rash of pink Bristols. One of a pair new in June 1969, it is seen in March 1970 on return to its home village, after working an American school's contract out of the nearby RAF Chicksands air base.

G. R. Mills

Plate 114: MEDIUM – Only five of the standard LH model were purchased for Taylor's superbly-maintained fleet. Mouldings and paintwork are always kept bright, whilst many older vehicles have had the seats reupholstered, even when only employed on contract work. No. 44 (VVD 44S), new in November 1977, was the last 45 seat Supreme LH supplied to the Bedfordshire operator, and still looked like new in this October 1978 'at home' view. A burgundy band had been introduced on this coach, a colour which was to gain momentum in the fleet livery, as *Plate 115* shows.

G. R. Mills

Plate 115: SMALL – Seemingly, the last new LHS body was to be the one outshopped by Plaxtons at Scarborough for Bere Regis Coaches, in March 1983. However, East Anglia's keenest LH owner was to upstage this claim. Purchasing an ex-London Country LHS with a burnt out ECW bus body, initially for chassis/engine spares, the decision was made to refurbish, update and eventually rebody the sound steel frame. Accordingly, the chassis was dispatched to Plaxtons (Southern) depot at Ware, (originally Thurgoods Works) to receive a new Supreme coach body. Work on the body was protracted over many months as urgent accident-damaged vehicles were repaired, until the completed 33 seat coach finally emerged in March 1984. New in September 1974 as XPD 124N, the vehicle was recertified as such, but gained a cherished SMJ 521 mark, in time to attend the 30th British Coach Rally at Brighton, held in April 1984. Appropriately, Taylors, 'Reliance' of Meppershall, Beds. was the only Bristol in the event which attracted over 80 entries, and it is seen arriving at Madeira Drive, after the road run, and prior to the driving tests.

G. R. Mills

A LITTLE BUNCH OF HARRISMENT AT GRAYS

The smart fleet of duo green coaches of Frank Harris (Coaches) Ltd., has, for many years, included heavyweight chassis. In the late 1950s and early 1960s the most popular choice was the AEC Reliance, whilst the Leyland Leopard was favoured in the late 1960s/early 1970s. The first Volvos arrived in 1973, followed by a rash of DAFs, delivery of which commenced in 1978. By this time the fleet included examples of AEC, Bristol, Leyland and Volvo; all the principal heavyweight coach chassis makes which were then available.

Plate 116 (above): Harris first invested in an LHS in 1975, delivery of which was effected in April. JVW 425N is sandwiched between two Volvos in a block of three registration numbers. It is seen in the Parker Road, Grays, parking area, in February 1980, by which time the 28 seater was for sale following the arrival of FTW 133T *(see Plate 118)*.

G. R. Mills

Plate 117 (right): The second Harris LHS was fitted with the roof destination box, popularly known in the trade as a 'Bristol dome'. New in June 1976, NEV 106P (again in a clutch of three consecutive numbers with two Volvos) is seen in Stratford-upon-Avon in July 1977.

G. R. Mills

Plate 118 (left): The third and final new LHS, which was delivered in May 1979, was fitted with a Plaxton Supreme body, as the previous pair. FTW 133T was among a block of four new coaches, and the remaining trio were DAF/Plaxtons. It is pictured in January 1980 emerging from the gloom of the original Parker Road garage, suitable for Bedford OB size vehicles, and the regular habitat of the LHS.

G. R. Mills

A BOON TO COACHING . . . AN LHL, LH AND LHS

Plate 119: In order to replace two Bedford VALs with more modern coaches, Boon's of Boreham, near Chelmsford, acquired a pair of LHLs. All four had Plaxton coachwork. The earlier VAL was Leyland-powered as were both the replacement vehicles. UAR 929M was new to Richardson, t/a Sheenway Coaches, London SW14, in May 1974 and carried a pink livery (as the company was originally owned by Taylor's, Meppershall). It passed to H. G. Boon when exactly three years old, and is seen in Chelmsford in January 1980.

G. R. Mills

Plate 120: Following the successful operation of two LHLs, Boon's ordered a new LH with a Plaxton Supreme 45 seat body. Delivered as WJN 22S, in February 1978, it was fitted with many extras, including a continental type step which is actuated by the main entrance door. This is an invaluable aid to senior citizens, and makes the use of the upturned box unnecessary. It is seen at Boreham, two months after delivery, showing the special step feature in operation.

G. R. Mills

Plate 121: Only two months later, and hard on the heels of the LH, came the LHS, also with Plaxton Supreme body but only seating 33. Both coaches were in the traditional deep red and cream livery, but with a clementine band. Both the LH and the LHS were sold after four years service in 1981. The same year also saw the sale of the LHL (*Plate 119*), and thus ended Bristol operation by Boon's.

G. R. Mills

An LHL, LH and LHS prove to be a further coaching BOON!

Plate 122: The last Bristol to leave the Boon fold was UAR 929M, which was sold in December 1981 to J. J. Watts, t/a Thurrock Coaches of Chadwell St. Mary, Essex. Retaining Boon's smart livery, but adding large lettering, the coach was seen on a school's swimming bath contract at Tilbury in April 1982, working to a sports complex at Grays.

G. R. Mills

Plate 123: WJN 22S was sold early in 1981 to Clarke of London SE3, who operates as both Brentons of Blackheath and Woodside Coaches. It is pictured in October 1983, arriving at the Rowley Mile Racecourse at Newmarket for the annual Cambridgeshire meeting. The coach has been repainted in a different style; black, cream, red, cream and black (reading upwards). A lively load of punters anxious to place their bets, are standing ready to leave before the vehicle comes to rest.

G. R. Mills

Plate 124: YVW 902S was found at a very different gathering in March 1982. when seen at Wembley Stadium. It is in town for the schoolboys' international football match, an event which attracts a vast amount of coach transport. Repainted in cream with a maroon band, for the very smart fleet of Chivers of Elstead, Surrey, it is in company with BNO 692T an Eastern National Bedford YMT/ Duple 53 seater, which has since been sold.

G. R. Mills

WESTWARDS FROM LONDON

Plate 125: Golden Miller of Feltham, Middlesex, already had ten LHs with coach bodies when their first bus example was delivered in November 1969. A prototype LHX chassis (No. 002), originally intended to have the 1968 show model body by Strachans of Hamble, was eventually bodied by Plaxtons with a 49 seat Derwent style body. CJJ 44H is seen at Feltham Station in May 1970, having worked in from Bedfont, on a service acquired from Tourist Coachways in 1966.

G. R. Mills

Plate 126: Blue Saloon of Guildford, Surrey, commenced stage carriage service work in March 1973 with a trio of ex-London RF type (Regal IV) buses. Ten years later, the bus fleet included a trio of LH vehicles with ECW bodies. Two were new, the first of which, KPB 881P, was supplied in October 1975. It is seen boldly displaying 'Weyfarer', the NBC local identity name, and is smartly attired in an ivory and deep blue livery, in keeping with the remainder of the fleet of 18 vehicles operated in April 1983.

G. R. Mills

Plate 127: Hutchings & Cornelius of South Petherton, Somerset, were keen operators of AEC Reliance/Willowbrook buses on their services to Yeovil and Taunton. In January 1972, this post-war allegiance was diverted to Bristol/ECW products, with the first LH with an ECW body delivered to an independent. A second model of the same combination was supplied a year later, as NYD 440L, in the H&C maroon and cream livery, and is seen in its home village in June 1976. Three years later, after the company ceased trading, the vehicle passed to Safeway, a neighbouring operator, who also acquired some of H&C commitments.

G. R Mills

EAST KENT ⇌ SHUTTLES

In post-war years, East Kent has consistently operated batches of diminutive buses. Initially, during 1949/50, Dennis Falcons replaced pre-war Dennis Aces on rural routes. In 1967 these were displaced by Bedford VASI models with Marshall Cambrette bodies. In July 1975, a new breed of 'baby buses' emerged, as four LHS vehicles with special ECW low profile bodies, for service under Newtown rail bridge, worked by Ashford depot.

Plate 128 (above): When exactly six years old, No. 1559 (GFN 559N), in standard NBC poppy red, is seen in Folkestone bus station, with 'On hire to British Rail' displayed on the destination blind.

D. G. Savage

Plate 129 (right): GFN 562N was employed almost exclusively on British Rail work from June 1977 when it received the Sealink livery of white and BR blue. It is seen in Folkestone bus station in April 1980.

M. Fowler

Plate 130 (left): No. 1560 (GFN 560N) is also seen in Folkestone bus station, but in August 1981, with an eye-catching livery adopted by Sealink as part of their measures to keep apace with the extensive competition for cross-channel traffic. The extremely colourful layout of basic white with red lid, plus four shades of blue skirt bands to represent the sea, gained an award in the annual Commercial Motor magazine livery competition.

D. G. Savage

HANTS & DORSET ON THE COURTESY TRAIL

Hants & Dorset were early pioneers of the LH chassis for bus work, and the first arrived in December 1968. Two years later, 26 were in service with ECW bodies, but with unusual two door configuration and a standee facility licensed for 12 persons. A further eight were supplied to the associated Wilts & Dorset fleet in the same period.

Plates 131 & 132: RLJ 794H was new in February 1970 as No. 3034, but by the time the upper view was taken of the bus arriving at Southampton bus station, in July 1972, still in its original livery, it had been renumbered 1530. In July 1977, it was transferred from Salisbury (ex-Wilts & Dorset depot) to the associated Gosport & Fareham fleet as No. 48, and carried 'Provincial' fleetnames, where it only survived for a year before its final withdrawal from NBC service. It was sold by Hants & Dorset in October 1978 to Martins (dealers) of Middlewich. By February 1982, when the lower view was taken in a general vehicle dealer's yard in Cranfield, Bedfordshire, it had survived another short career as a hospitality vehicle for the Windshields Group of Coventry. The plain all white paintwork, apart from logos, has transformed the exterior, whilst the interior has been altered to perimeter seating with a even larger standee area than originally-allocated when new.

D. G. Savage & G. R. Mills

Plate 133: Another member of the 26 dual-doored LHs to gain longevity is REL 743H. It is one of a pair retained by Hants & Dorset after their PSV life as towing wagons. It was renumbered from 1522 to 9079 for its non-PSV duties at Fareham, and was acquired by Eastern Counties in late 1982 and converted into an attactive mobile advertising media vehicle. It has been repainted into a basic cream livery, with numerous slogans and colourful diagrams to promote many aspects of the company's operations, and is pictured at the Norfolk Showground, in September 1983, attending the highly-successful British Bus weekend, organised by the Eastern Counties Omnibus Society.

G. R. Mills

Plate 134: All the ECW-bodied dual doorway LH buses built were supplied to Hants & Dorset/Wilts & Dorset. RLJ 744H, one of the first batch which was delivered in 1969, is seen after transfer to Gosport & Fareham 'Provincial', managed by Hants & Dorset from January 1970. This vehicle had the special task and stickers for a free service to the local Asda superstore when seen at Gosport in July 1978.

M. A. Penn

Plate 135: From 1973-5, Hants & Dorset took delivery of 85 LH buses with ECW 43 seat bodies. By the end of 1983, all had been withdrawn from passenger carrying duties. In their wake came 42 similar vehicles of 1978-80 vintage from Bristol Omnibus Co., and 30 ex-London DMS class Daimler Fleetline double deckers. This example was retained for conversion to a tree lopper, on which work was in an advanced state when seen in the central works at Eastleigh in November 1982. The bus had previously been available for use on the Poole to Sandbanks Ferry — hence the cutaway front lower panel work. The vehicle was later allocated to the Poole depot of the Wilts & Dorset Bus Co., which was formed in April 1983.

G. R. Mills

Plate 136: Allocation to the coaching division of Hants & Dorset meant that the unique 1982 charabanc passed to Shamrock & Rambler Coaches Ltd., formed in April 1983, for use on specialised and publicity work. Originally a standard ECW-bodied 43 seat bus, new in 1974 as NLJ 516M, it was the subject of a massive rebuild to the form seen at Holdenhurst Road depot, Bournemouth, in June 1983. The cherished registration was originally carried on a 1929 Leyland PLSC with Leyland 35 seat body, new to Hants & Dorset subsequently passing to Wilts & Dorset and finally being scrapped in April 1943. The lined-out green livery resembles that of the original vehicle.

G. R. Mills

EX-HANTS & DORSET MOVE TO ESSEX

Plate 137: The purchase of thirty ex-London Transport DMS class Daimler Fleetline double deckers from Ensign, dealers, Purfleet, Essex, ousted the bulk of the last LHs which had been supplied new to Hants & Dorset. LJT 940P, one of the final batch of six, originally diverted from Southdown, is seen at Basildon on 1st January 1983 en route to be sampled by a PSV customer.

G. R. Mills

Plate 138: The customer proved to be the long-established Essex stage carriage operator G. W. Osborne & Sons, Tollesbury. As past owners of three Leyland Tiger Cubs, with the economical 400 unit, the chance to acquire a trio of LHs with ECW bodies in very good condition, powered by a similar Leyland 401 unit, was welcomed. LJT 940P is seen in Tiptree, in March 1983, fully repainted in duo red and white, bound for the rail station terminus to collect London commuters.

G. R. Mills

Plate 139: The final vehicle in the final Hants & Dorset batch had also received a full repaint in this February 1983 photograph. It is seen on Ensign's 15 acre site at Purfleet, having been transformed into NBC white coach livery, albeit not for such duties! The vehicle was prepared for export to Oman, a country beside the Arabian Sea; a vast contrast to the English Channel resorts of its original operations! The final night in England was spent in the company of a Welsh Leyland Atlantean/Alexander double decker (ex-Newport) and a Scottish Bristol Lodekka (ex-Western SMT).

G. R. Mills

VODKA EXCELL in ESSEX

Plate 140: Amongst Western National's vast intake of LH models were a dozen LHS/Marshalls and fourteen LH/ECW buses with VOD-K registration marks. Often dubbed the 'vodka' batch, the vehicles were supplied in 1972. No. 1586 (VOD 117K), is shown at Taunton in June 1982, in the twilight of its career in the Western National fleet.

D. G. Savage

Plate 141 As with Hants & Dorset, many Western National LH buses found their way to Ensign, dealer, of Purfleet, as part-exchange vehicles for ex-London DMS double deckers. Thus VOD 117K was supplied to Smith & May, t/a S&M Coaches and Castlepoint Bus Co., Benfleet, Essex, in March 1983. Repainted red and cream for schools and contract duties, it is seen in October 1983 at rest at a Corringham café.

G. R. Mills

Plate 142: The LH found instant favour at S&M, such that a second model entered service the following month. The twin was this refugee from Hants & Dorset. Again part of sixteen in a single registration block delivered during 1971/2, 'Excell' XEL 831K varied from the Western National example on various fittings such as 'Pay as you Enter' panels and the emergency door valve/button, although the principal frontal feature is the twin headlamps, as seen at Southchurch Park, Southend, in June 1983.

G. R. Mills

BRISTOLS RETURN TO Bristol

Plate 143: Nine of Thames Valley's first twenty LH buses went to United Automobile Services, whilst five went to the Bristol Omnibus Co. VMO 227H, seen here at rest in Maidenhead bus station in April 1970, was one of the latter which moved back to its birthplace city in 1977.

D. G. Savage

Plate 144: Acquired from the Alder Valley fleet in February 1977, the vehicle has lost its cream window surrounds in favour of a white waistband, as shown in this May 1977 view, as the bus enters Malborough Street bus station in Bristol. After its sale in 1980, the vehicle saw further service with Pullman Kellogg, main contractors on the Mobil oil refinery extension at Canvey Island, Essex.

G. R. Mills

Plate 145: Windmill Hill Community bus is a special service, with an LH in a special livery, which operates in South Bristol. It serves Windmill Hill (as the name suggests) and Totterdown areas, via narrow roads in hilly terrain. On Mondays to Fridays, the bus provides a local link to the health centre, an hourly facility to Bedminster shopping area, plus peak hour journeys to and from the city centre. No. 305 (RPH 108L), seen at Broad Quay terminus in the city, in April 1983, is one of a pair acquired from London Country in 1980, and is attired in the attractive green and white Windmill Hill livery.

G. R. Mills

BRISTOL LH
A BUS FOR ALL DEPOTS

Bristol Omnibus Company's LH buses have seen service at all the company's depots within their extensive operating area. Bath, Cheltenham, Gloucester, Stroud, Swindon, Wells and Weston-super-Mare have all operated examples of the 116 LHs taken into stock.

Plate 146: The second LH of the first batch supplied to Bristol Omnibus Co., No. 352 (DHW 292K), is seen in the livery adopted for one-man-operated vehicles. The batch was unique, as the paint style had no green skirt, and they were Bristol Omnibus Company's only semi-automatic transmission LHs. It is captured at rest in September 1973, in the bus station/garage at Weston-super-Mare, the company's busiest seasonal depot.

A. MacFarlane

Plate 147: Numerically the second vehicle of the third batch, No. 366 (KHU 316P), is seen entering the old Swindon bus station in August 1980. In the background a Thamesdown Daimler Fleetline/MetCam (159) passes by, bound for the town centre. Note the British Rail logo on the opposite end of the building displaying Hambro Life.

G. R. Mills

Plate 148: The last LH built was appropriately supplied to Bristol Omnibus Co., in 1980, with the traditional ECW 43 seat bus body. AFB 597V, as No. 466 of MH (Marlborough Street, Bristol) depot, sets off for Weston-super-Mare in April 1983, closely followed by a Bath vehicle, No. 2060, an RELH6L, another type which has now sadly been discontinued after a highly successful career.

G. R. Mills

THAMES VALLEY

Thames Valley was the principal stage carriage operator in Royal Berkshire, based on Reading, with three other depots in the county at Bracknell, Maidenhead and Newbury, plus High Wycombe in Buckinghamshire. From 1950-71, the coaching division used the South Midland fleetname, thus the first LHs supplied to the company in 1968, which had Duple Commander III C41F bodies, were delivered in cream with brown bands, rather than in Tilling red and cream, for the coach fleet. Control of South Midland passed, together with the twelve LHs, to City of Oxford Motor Services.

Plates 149, 150 & 151: The first batch of LH buses supplied to Thames Valley were eight ECW B45F vehicles delivered in 1969 as RRX 991-8G, illustrated by No. 201 (RRX 992G) *(top)* seen turning into Maidenhead bus station in April 1969. No. 513 (RRX 993G) is seen at High Wycombe in the later livery in September 1976, *(centre)* and has obviously had problems! In 1977, these vehicles and three others of the same batch passed to United Automobile Services, joining five newer examples which had gone north the previous year. However, one of the batch came southwards again, as far as East Anglia, when David List of Debenham, Suffolk, purchased RRX 993G from Twell, (dealer) of Ingham, Linconlnshire, for a schools contract. Operating in the Eastern Counties area, the vehicle was repainted so as not to be confused with a company bus. The colour chosen was a deep maroon, not unlike the livery of Alder Valley's short-lived original colour scheme. It is seen *(below)* on the owner's garage forecourt in July 1981.

G. R. Mills, D. G. Savage & G. R. Mills

Thamesdown Transport

Plates 152 & 153: Swindon, famed as a railway town, has, in post-war years, been a stronghold for Daimler buses, all supplied new. In saloon deliveries AEC Reliances broke the monopoly in 1963, followed by Leyland Leopards in 1967 and Bristol RE/ECW models in 1975. The first second-hand vehicles in the undertaking's history, renamed Thamesdown Transport in April 1974, were taken into stock in 1983. Three 1976 LH6L/ECW ex-London Transport vehicles were the pioneer used saloons, which blended well with the RE/ECWs which were still in stock. No. 41 (OJD 68R) is seen with one of the six ex-London DMS Fleetlines which were acquired for extra school contracts. All nine share the OJD-R series registration block, and the smart cream and blue livery. The ex-'Londoners' stand *(top)* in part of the new bus station under construction early 1984, and *(bottom)* No. 41 departs from the local leisure park at Coate Water, amidst frost-laden trees.

G. R. Mills

PIONEERS OF THE WEST

Plate 154: The first, not only to Western National, but numerically the first production LH built was No. 722 (MUO 334F), which has the exalted chassis No. 101. It is seen here at Taunton garage yard, in March 1977, wearing the second livery variant applied to the batch of fifteen delivered in 1968 (white band on the NBC leaf green basic hue).

S. J. Purkiss

Plate 155: The original style of livery is portrayed by No. 715 (MUO 327F) seen arriving at Penzance bus station in June 1976. The Western National fleetname, originally positioned amidships, has been obliterated by a lager advert. A second siting above the wheel arch is still vaguely visible, but has been painted out to comply with the NBC ruling of having the fleetname on the roof panels. The small fleetname carried on the front panel below the windscreen has also been painted out.

G. R. Mills

Plate 156: When this view was taken at New Covent Garden, Vauxhall, in September 1981, MUO 328F had found its way up into South-West London, via Ensign, the well-known Essex dealers, who supplied Western National with ex-London Daimler DMS class double deckers. One of the pioneer batch ironically was purchased by Continental Pioneer of Richmond, and smartly repainted in a blue livery. Note the rebuilt windscreen and destination box, which was completed whilst with Western National.

D. G. Savage

ROYAL BLUE

Coaching division of Southern/Western National since February 1935.

The fleetname Royal Blue was once synonymous with dark blue-liveried luxury coaches providing express services to Bournemouth and the West Country. A variation from the superb comfort offered by the generously-spaced seating of the Bristol L, LS, MW and RE models was provided by varied LH batches, also with reduced maximum seating capacities.

Plate 157: No. 1304 (RDV 439H), a 1970 example with a Duple Commander C41F body, is seen at Windsor Safari Park in May 1972. These were the first coach-bodied LHs supplied to the Western National group.

G. R. Mills

Plate 158: For the second batch of LH coaches, the body order went to Plaxtons. Although a familiar combination in the private sector, apart from the Western National group only United had an identical batch of coaches. No. 1314 (UTT 580J), one of four, new in 1971, is seen leaving Victoria Coach Station in April 1974. The vehicle has worked in from Bristol and is about to visit Samuelsons garage for a refuel and oil/water check.

G. R. Mills

Plate 159: The third batch of Royal Blue coaches with LH-chassis, were the most startling choice of the ten with Marshall of Cambridge coachwork. Functional if somewhat austere in styling, Marshall were more associated with bus bodywork. Delivered late in 1973, No. 1323 (NTT 323M) is seen at the Battersea Wharf NBC parking area in London, in June 1974.

G. R. Mills

A SQUEEZE DOWN THE MOUSEHOLE

A delightful Cornish fishing village with very narrow streets.

Plates 160, 161 & 162: A series of views photographed in June 1976, as the LHS arrives from Penzance bus station. No. 1255 (VOD 125K), one of a dozen new in 1972 with Marshall of Cambridge 33 seat bus bodies, squeezes down the main street to Mousehole harbour. The turn-round beside the war memorial is equally tight, and demands expert judgement by Western National drivers. The advertisement on the side panels exalts the virtues of a full strength lager with a truly individual flavour; issued to bus drivers to help them manhandle the LHS with no power-steering, as rum is to sailors, maybe? No doubt a very acceptable idea for Western National staff!

G. R. Mills

MORE VARIETY TO THE MOUSEHOLE

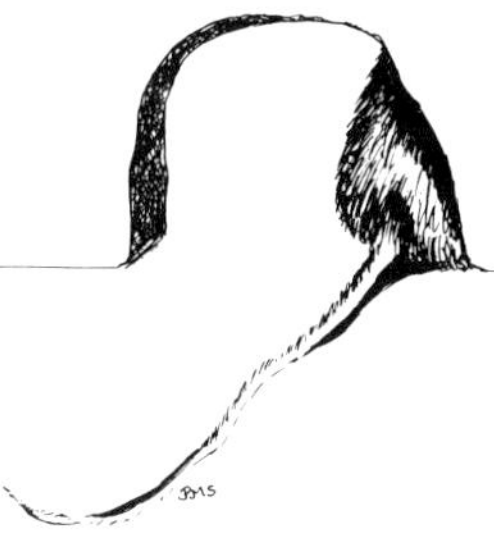

Plate 163: In post-war years the Penzance to Mousehole route has seen Bedford OB/Beadles replaced by Bristol SU vehicles, which in turn were ousted by the 7ft. 6in. wide LHS, both with Marshall (new 1972) and ECW (new 1979) bodies. One of the latter of a batch of eight, backs off the stand at Penzance bus station in May 1982, displaying the short-lived Cornish Fairways fleetname.

G. R. Mills

Plate 164: In keeping with the local NBC operator, the first LHS of Harvey's of Mousehole was bodied by Marshalls of Cambridge. Although the Western National examples were five years older than PCV 178R delivered in April 1977, the body style was virtually identical to that of its neighbours. It is seen arriving at Penzance bus station, in May 1982, in the independent's blue and white colours, strangely devoid of any modern fleetname.

G. R. Mills

Plate 165: KRL 444W is a unique vehicle, as it is the only Wadham Stringer-bodied LHS produced. This length of Vanguard body was also supplied to Eastern National on Bedford YMQS chassis. Harvey's have employed the bus on the Penzance service since September 1981. The smart blue and white bus is seen backed on to the stand in May 1982.

G. R. Mills

A MARSHALL OF THE WEST

Plate 166: The ten Marshalls were destined for a colourful career after their initial Royal Blue hue. The square box proportions of the body were more suited to bus type livery than coach styling, and No. 1319 (NTT 319M) is seen here as a Marshall of Dartmouth (sub-depot of Plymouth), in NBC white livery, with 'blue bib', at Mayors Avenue depot in June 1976.

G. R. Mills

Plate 167: Every American's idea of an English bus, generated by the London image, is always red. Despite well-known concerns rejoicing in colourful names like Blue Bus Services, Green Bus, and Yellow Bus Services, no sizeable operator in modern times has chosen the simple title 'Red Bus'. North Devon Ltd., formed in January 1983, have No. 1320 (NTT 320M) which was inherited with a variety of Western National stock. The Marshall of Barnstaple is seen at home in September 1983 smartly attired in its new livery.

D. G. Savage

Plate 168: The green livery of Western National suited the body shape well, as displayed by No. 1324 (NTT 324M) seen departing from Plymouth Bretonside bus station in June 1983. The Wayfarer ticket advert has, alas, interrupted the white waistband, spoiling the otherwise neat body lines. On being repainted into bus livery, both Marshalls have lost the fussy little 'flick-up' at the rear of the side mouldings *(see Plate 166)*. The bus is working a South Hams area route, which was formerly worked by Devon General vehicles.

D. G. Savage

WHAT'S A NAME?

Plate 169: Twelve vehicles, similar to the one shown, were originally supplied to Greenslades Tours Ltd. of Exeter, for the 1975 touring season. All were specially-constructed with 7ft. 6in. wide bodies, for use on the narrow Devon and Cornwall roads, and were registered JFJ 497-508N. When less than a year old, they returned to Plaxtons for frontal modification, to alleviate overheating problems. No. 320 (JFJ 500N) is pictured at the ex-Thurgood works, based at Widbury Hill, Ware, in April 1976, awaiting entry into the workshops prior to the conversion. The vehicle passed to Western National, as part of the first six of the batch in 1978.

G. R. Mills

Plate 170: The second half of the batch, JFJ 503-8N, were retained as National Travel (South West) Ltd. coaches until 1978, before transfer to Western National. No. 327 (JFJ 507N) is seen in September 1979 at Buckfast Abbey, Devon, a regular seasonal haunt for a vast number of coaches. Still based at the Greenslades depot in Exeter, the coach has acquired revised fleetnames. Note the rebuilt front grille arrangement for increased ventilation to the radiator, and also the loss of the wheel trims.

D. G. Savage

Plate 171: The final indignity for one of the first six, JFJ 502N, was the repainting into dual-purpose livery of NBC poppy red and white, and relegation to bus duties. Based at Newton Abbot depot, it is pictured on a local service to a housing estate from the adjoining bus station, in May 1983. Despite the livery and fleetname changes, the entire batch of twelve have always carried an Exeter address as the legal ownership which was appropriate to their registration mark origins.

D. G. Savage

A GENERAL LOOK AT LIVERIES ON DEVON LH COACHES

Plate 172: The last LH supplied to Western National was No. 3323 (AFJ 743T), fitted with a 7ft. 6in. wide version of Plaxton's Supreme Express body, seating 41. One of twenty four delivered in 1979, the illustration shows the coach in October of the same year, in NBC red and white, laden with young sailors at the Naval Dockyard at Chatham, about to return to a similar establishment at Devonport.

G. R. Mills

Plate 173: This view shows another livery worn by the LH/Plaxton Supreme combination, exemplified by No. 3118 (SFJ 118R), part of a batch of twenty six 8ft. wide bodied examples delivered in 1977. The vehicle is shown, in white livery with a broad red band, at rest in Exeter bus station before making a return trip to its home depot at Newton Abbot, in September 1983.

D. G. Savage

Plate 174: In 1983, the previous simplified liveries gave way to a trendy striped styling. No. 3322 (AFJ 742T) displays the freshly-applied Devon General version, at Torquay, in September 1983. Still in the basic white livery with a broad maroon band, the intricate stripes at the front half of the coach are grey; a modern version of the erstwhile Grey Cars coaching division of Devon General?

D. G. Savage

TWO EXTREMES

Plate 175: Due to the curious shape of the British Isles, the most Westerly and Southerly points in England lie within 34 miles of each other. Both of these coastal points are situated in Cornwall, and both are reached by Bristol LH vehicles. The western point, appropriately named Land's End, is served by Penzance-based Western National vehicles, as portrayed by No. 3401 (PTT 101R) departing the bus station (Motorail terminal in background) in May 1982. The Plaxton Supreme body, in the local coach green and white livery, is typical of a large intake on LH chassis.

G. R. Mills

N
CORNWALL
PLYMOUTH
PENZANCE
Lands End
FALMOUTH
The Lizard
ENGLISH CHANNEL

Plate 176: The southernmost point, The Lizard, takes its name from the Cornish 'lis' meaning place and 'ard' meaning high. This beauty spot is the haunt of the sparkling cream and orange buses operated by J. H. Pollard & Son of Ruan Minor, t/a Cherry Tree Coaches. KJD 421P, ex-London Transport, with a 7ft. 6in. wide ECW body is seen returning to base on a hot day in May 1982.

G. R. Mills

BRISTOLS IN BRETONSIDE

Plymouth's combined bus and coach station was opened at Bretonside in March 1958. Since that date, the site has daily been host to a wide variety of PSVs. Western National have consistently provided vehicles of Bristol manufacture in the form of LH models since 1968.

Plate 177: From July 1982, Plymouth City Transport introduced a striking new livery with the fleetname 'Citybus'. A surprise purchase of six ex-Western National LH buses, in September of the same year, also produced 'Countrybus' for vehicles venturing further afield in the reorganised Joint Services Area. No. 19 (NFJ 592M), one of three from the same 1973 batch acquired, is seen in Bretonside on arrival from Buckland and Milton Combe in June 1983. A Western National Bristol RE is seen at the rear.

D. G. Savage

Plate 178: The largest independent stage operator in the Plymouth area is Tally Ho! with vehicles based in the city. Having purchased two ex-London Country LHS models in 1981, which proved to be ideal vehicles for the operation of stage services on Devon roads, the company further invested in a pair of larger LH versions which were formerly owned by London Transport. OJD 58R is seen about to depart from Bretonside with a lively load of old age pensioners in September 1982, its first month in the West Country. The livery application has similarly moved from the layer style to a modern impact design. In the background KVO 147W, a Trent Leyland Leopard/Willowbrook coach, waits to work an express service to Nottingham, via Bristol and Birmingham.

D. G. Savage

CORNISH LHs

'The Cornishman' fleet, from Wadebridge, has school journeys in the Bodmin area on stage licences, in addition to a May to October Newquay town service.

Plate 179: RDV 436H, seen in May 1982, is one of a pair of ex-Royal Blue LH coaches which stayed in their own old territory. Part of a rare batch fitted with Duple Commander bodies, Barry Gill Motors have retained the Royal Blue style paint layout, but have replaced the blue with maroon (not unlike the shade once used by South Midland).

G. R. Mills

Plate 180: Barry Gill Motors' expansion began with the acquisition, in January 1982, of Hubber, Streamline Coaches, Newquay, which included the above LH, joining a twin already in use. Further commitments were added with the full-sized coaches and contracts of Martyn, J. M. Coaches, St. Columb Major, which included a 1973 LH/Plaxton Elite Express, new to Silcox of Pembroke Dock, adding to the growing fleet of LH models in operation. On this occasion, GDE 374L is approaching Pentire Head, in Newquay, on a cool day in October 1983. The Bristol dome is used to full advantage to display the 'Cornishman' fleetname.

S. J. Purkiss

Plate 181: Barry Gill Motors' earlier experience of LHL operation prompted the purchase of JAF 635N, supplied new in July 1975. The 45 seat Plaxton Elite Express III bodied coach is well beyond its local habitat, in this September 1978 view, whilst on tour on the Isle of Wight. The customary upturned wooden crate, to aid old folks' entry into the vehicle, is prominently visible!

G. R. Mills

FIRST AND LAST OF THE LHS

Plate 182: The first LHS was to remain a unique bus. The only one with an F suffix registration, the only one supplied to Western Welsh, and the only one to receive a second-hand body. The company experimented by having a Weymann 30 seat bus body removed from a seven year old Albion Nimbus (WKG 27), and the resulting vehicle was registered MBO 1F. The hybrid is seen at Cardiff bus station in May 1973. Four years later the special left Wales for a new owner in Yorkshire, Thorne's Motor Services, Bubwith, near Selby.

G. R. Mills

Plate 183: The last LHS chassis, No. 408, indicating 308 production models, as the numbering commenced at 101. It was supplied to the well-known West Country stage carriage operator, Bere Regis & District of Dorchester, in their traditional duo brown and red livery. CLJ 413Y was fitted with Plaxton Supreme V coachwork, and is seen departing from the narrow access to the trading estate at Wimborne, Dorset, in June 1983, where the company have a small depot.

G. R. Mills

Welsh Wee ones

The two LHS vehicles in the City of Cardiff fleet represent a mere one per cent of the total vehicle strength. LUH 104P and 105P were new in June 1976, and had ECW bodies fitted with 27 semi-luxury seats. They are attired in a rich orange livery and, like the remainder of the fleet, carry the Welsh capital's title in English on the nearside and in the native tongue on the offside.

Plate 184 (above): No. 104 (LUH 104P) passes the Welsh Empire Pool in January 1978.

D. G. Savage

Plate 185 (left): No. 105 (LUH 105P) is seen near the Civic Centre in July 1977.

G. R. Mills

Plate 186 (right): Four more LH/ECW vehicles (ex-London Country) were purchased by Cardiff in later years. This was not the only London area LH penetration into Welsh municipal operations. The Rhymney Valley DC of Caerphilly decided three of these useful-sized buses could be utilised on their services in the valleys. Former No. BL45 (OJD 45R), working out of Hengoed depot, is seen in July 1983 at Bute Town, in the unusual brown, ochre and cream livery adopted by the Cyngor Ardal Cwm Rhymni.

R. J. Hefford

A TRIO OF WELSH RARE BITS

Plate 187: A Plaxton Derwent 52 seat body was fitted to JCY 478N, an LH6L, new in 1975 to Jones of Carmarthen, who purchased four other bus-bodied LHs for the town services, taken over from Western Welsh in 1971. Control of the Jones business passed to Davies Bros. in April 1978, together with all the rolling stock, which included two Plaxton 45 seat coaches and a rare Duple 35 seat coach on an LH6L chassis. Davies No. 118 (ex-Jones No. 8) is seen at the ex-Jones Abergwili garage in June 1980.

G. R. Mills

Plate 188: The body on the first LH in the Davies, Pencader, fleet is ECW-built. The familiar NBC style vehicle, in red and cream livery, was new in April 1975. It is pictured, in July 1977, circumnavigating the bus station in Carmarthen. HBX 948N has a bold fleet number, 97.

G. R. Mills

Plate 189: A Duple Dominant bus body on an LH6L makes No. 98 (KBX 38P) a very rare vehicle. With chassis number and fleet number consecutive with the vehicle in *Plate 188,* the five months later delivery gave rise to the change in registration letter suffix. No. 98 is seen at the Blossom garage forecourt, Pencader, in June 1980.

G. R. Mills

WELSH STAGE WORK
BY PLAXTONS

Plate 190: The well-known Silcox of Pembroke Dock, Dyfed, fleet has long been synonymous with Bristol chassis. The post-war years have seen most types surplus from BTC/NBC group sources on Silcox work. Not surprisingly two LHs were purchased new in July 1969. These were fitted with Plaxton Derwent bus bodies incorporating 43 semi-luxury seats. RDE 660G, one of the pair, seen on a very warm day in July 1977, has some non-standard frontal trim additives.

G. R. Mills

Plate 191: Llynfi Motor Services of Maesteg in Mid Glamorgan have long been a Leyland-biased fleet. The two LH buses supplied with Plaxton Derwent bodies, in April 1973, were seemingly non-standard, although the Leyland 401 power unit brought the pair closer to the main fleet. Seen at the main depot yard, which is set high above the town, the smart blue and cream bus had just returned after a day's service work.

G. R. Mills

Plate 192: Coity Motors, of Coity in Mid Glamorgan, have a small fleet of stage vehicles, which are regularly seen in nearby Bridgend. Unfortunately, ATG 459H, a unique LHL6L Plaxton Derwent 55 seater, and the only LHL to receive a bus body, will be seen no more; a disastrous fire destroyed the vehicle in September 1983. It is seen here, in happier times, parked after a day's work in the valleys, in June 1980.

G. R. Mills

THREE LITTLE WISHES . . . GRANTED

Plate 193: Wembley Stadium is a mecca for large volumes of coaching names from a wide spectrum of locations. This June 1983 scene shows an ex-Welsh-based LHS arriving for the schoolboys' international football match, and is seen passing a parked Bedford YRT, new to the Tyne & Wear area. The Bristol has only travelled from South-East London with its 33 seat load of young males. Operated by Clark, t/a Birds of Blackheath since mid-1979, it was joined by a brand-new example from the same operator's 'Woodside' fleet in October 1980.

G. R. Mills

Plate 194: Special operating conditions could enable an operator to obtain a new bus grant on vehicles not included in the standard specifications set by the Ministry of Transport. The LH, with an ECW bus body, was typical of the normally-accepted smallest in the range of single deck high floor buses at 9 metres long. However, three LHS models were bodied in 1975 with **grant** doors, to the **wish** of S. A. Bebb Ltd., of Llantwit Fadre in Glamorgan, by Plaxtons. HKG 66N in white, gold and black livery is seen in Cardiff bus station in July 1977 awaiting a return load to Beddau.

G. R. Mills

Plate 195: Of the trio, HKG 67N was the one to constantly change hands, whereas its stablemates left Bebb and stayed with one owner for at least four years. HKG 67N initially went to Pilchers, Chatham, Kent, thence to Allans of Keyston, Hunts., with whom it is seen on a council-sponsored service into St. Neots in July 1980. Although attractively repainted into orange, cream and black, from green, it survived only a year on 'Stagecoach' work before being replaced. By mid-1982, it was back on stage services into Hitchin, with Smiths of Buntingford, Herts., in white and blue livery, but twenty months later, it was 'exported' to Cork in Southern Ireland, to join its sixth owner.

G. R. Mills

A CHASSIS NEEDS . . . SOMEBODY SOMETIME!

Plate 196: Bristol LHS6L chassis No. 302 was exhibited at the 1976 Commercial Motor Show, at Earls Court in London, as illustrated in this September 1976 high level view. The chassis entered service, complete with a 33 seat Plaxton Supreme coach body, in April 1977 as RDW 45R with J. M. Crookes, t/a Wenallt Coaches, Rhiwbina, in Cardiff. This replaced a similar vehicle which the operator had purchased two years previously (HUH 460N).

A. Macfarlane

Plate 197: Early in 1978, the long-established Wiffens, from the picturesque Essex village of Finchingfield, were seeking a superior vehicle to replace a Bedford VAS on pop group work. The opportunity to buy an eleven month old LHS was seized as the Wenallt coach fleet had ceased to trade and RDW 45R was available. In post-war years, it was to be the only coach operated by Wiffens that was not repainted in their attractive duo green and white. Seen in its second home base, very early on a misty April 1978 morning, on a short rest before tours, it is still in original duo brown livery.

G. R. Mills

Plate 198: After two seasons on pop tours, the LHS was replaced by a new Ford (shortened by Tricentrol), and the vehicle moved on yet again. Still less than three years old when acquired by Herberts of Shefford, Beds., ironically it joined its older brother, HUH 460N, which it had ousted in Wales. In the interim period, the older LHS had logged colossal mileage on journeys through Europe to Asia and North Africa before being reunited, and they were both repainted into an attractive red, white and black livery as Herbert's two big coaches in a fleet of minibuses. The side slogan reads 'Small party travel! It must be HERBERTS'.

G. R. Mills

NATIONAL WELSH

Although various models produced by Bristol Commercial Vehicles found their way into the Welsh NBC fleets (i.e. Red & White, Chepstow; South Wales Transport, and Western Welsh collectively had LS, MW, RE and SU saloons), no batches of LH variants were ever ordered by the 'big three'. A solitary experimental LHS was purchased in 1967, but it was not until after National Welsh was formed, in April 1978, from Red & White, Western Welsh and Jones of Aberbeeg, that two batches of Bristol LHS made their debut for the model.

Plate 199: One of the first batch of six awaits collection at ECW at Lowestoft in Suffolk, in November 1980. GTX 760W has the National arrow-head logo, but no fleetname or number, which were to be applied on arrival in Wales. Finished in local coach livery (dual-purpose poppy red and white), the vehicles were fitted with 27 seats with head-rests.

D. G. Savage

Plate 200: Of the six 1980 deliveries, two were allocated to Aberdare, whilst the remainder were despatched to Porth depot in the Rhondda. Of the latter, two were painted in a startling blue and yellow livery for a new type of Community Bus Service. Sponsored by Mid Glamorgan CC., the service offers a hail and ride facility where it diverts from roads served by other bus routes. No. MD8023, (GTX 758W) the first of the batch, is seen about to leave Porth depot, in September 1982, followed by a standard 1978 Leyland National.

G. R. Mills

THE CHANNEL ISLANDS
GBJ and GBG

Plates 201 & 202: The surplus LHs from London Transport are ideal for Channel Islands' operation, in view of their narrow and short proportions. OJD 12R, seen at Ensign's paintshops when based at Grays, had just received duo brown livery in this May 1982 view. It is appropriately in the company of an RT class double decker, prior to its 'export' to Jersey, initially for the conveyance of film crews in connection with the well-known 'Bergerac' TV film series. It is also pictured re-registered J29184 and is seen on the quayside at St. Helier in September 1983, little changed apart from the addition of curtains.

G. R. Mills

Plate 203: The ECW invasion of Guernsey began in 1980 by the acquisition of numerous ex-Western National SUL4A vehicles to replace the aged fleet of Albion Victors. Shortly before Christmas 1983, the first of a dozen ex-London Transport ECW-bodied LHs arrived on the island. Former No. BL 43 (OJD 43R) was used on driver familiarisation, initially in a white livery, but it was repainted red prior to its release on to normal public service workings. It is seen as No. 61 (9439) on a grey and overcast day in February 1984, attractively attired in an all-over advertising livery for Barclays Bank, with one of the earlier Lowestoft-built bodies on an SUL4A. No. 136 (31909) was originally EDV 537D.

J. Carman

SOUTHERN VECTIS

Plate 204: LDL 262F is a registration mark that would have been highly appropriate on a Lodekka! It is one of a pair of LHs delivered in 1968, fitted with Leyland 401 engines. Many of the early models had Perkins engines and the early style shallow windscreen ECW 43 seat body. It is seen arriving at Ryde Esplanade, from Newport, in May 1974, wearing the final unrelieved all green livery. Both these pioneers passed to United Automobile Services in July 1977.

D. G. Savage

Plate 205: The last of the breed, No. 204 (KDL 204W), was one of a trio of LHS vehicles delivered in November 1980. It is fitted with neat ECW body with 31 semi-luxury seats, which, with additional exterior side mouldings plus the dual-purpose livery, presents a smart vehicle, and it is seen arriving at Newport bus station on a very local service in August 1982.

D. G. Savage

COWES
RYDE
YARMOUTH
NEWPORT
ISLE OF WIGHT
SANDOWN
SHANKLIN
VENTNOR

NORTH AND SOUTH OF THE FRIENDLY ISLE

Plate 206: Southern Vectis were early purchasers of the LHS, being rivalled only by Lincolnshire for the first production models. The four taken into stock were the first bodied by Marshall of Cambridge. No. 834 (NDL 770G), seen in what appears to be a local hostelry, has, in fact, turned from Cowes main street under the archway to the Pontoon terminus. The small body dimensions of 26ft. by 7ft. 6in. were essential to this manoeuvre. The photograph was taken in September 1978 when the condition of the bus belied its ten year vintage.

G. R. Mills

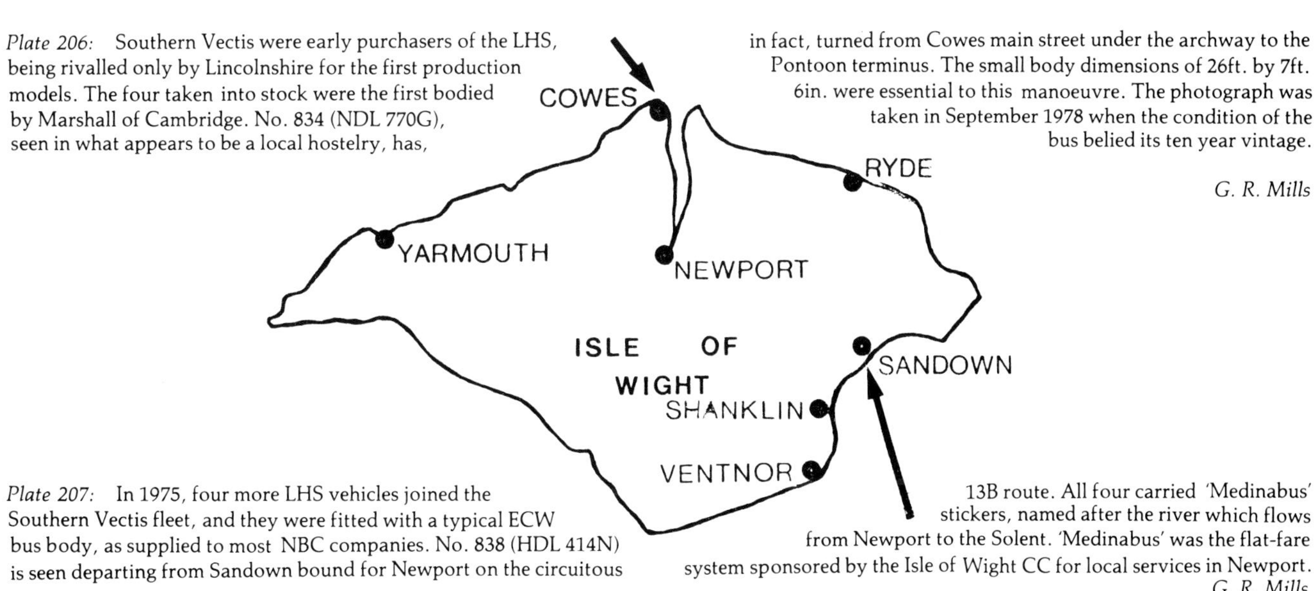

Plate 207: In 1975, four more LHS vehicles joined the Southern Vectis fleet, and they were fitted with a typical ECW bus body, as supplied to most NBC companies. No. 838 (HDL 414N) is seen departing from Sandown bound for Newport on the circuitous 13B route. All four carried 'Medinabus' stickers, named after the river which flows from Newport to the Solent. 'Medinabus' was the flat-fare system sponsored by the Isle of Wight CC for local services in Newport.

G. R. Mills

BIG NAMES IN COACHING

Plate 208: Wallace Arnold Tours, Leeds, is probably the best-known and largest touring coach fleet in the country, apart from NBC combined totals. As part of Devon operations, based on Paignton, the Embankment fleetname is perpetuated for work out of Plymouth. HWU 85N, one of six LH/Plaxton Elite 45 seaters, new in 1975, is seen on the quayside at Looe, Cornwall, in June 1976.

G. R. Mills

Plate 209: The large London-based Grey-Green Coaches have been connecting East Anglia to the capital with express services for over fifty years. In post-war years, the Leyland mark has reigned supreme from PS1 and PS2, through Royal Tiger, Tiger Cub, to Leopard and the new breed of Tiger. Several batches of Bedfords have been purchased, the majority fitted with Leyland units. The first Bristols (three LHL and one LH) were delivered in April 1969 with Plaxton bodies and Leyland engines (of course!). AGH 590G, the Ewer Group's first LH, is seen returning from Clacton on an Essex Coast Express, on a Sunday evening in June 1970. The service was then jointly-operated with the now defunct Suttons Coaches.

G. R. Mills

Plate 210: WLT 579G was one of the trio of LHLs, supplied to Grey-Green in 1969, concurrently with the coach seen in *Plate 209.* WLT 578-80G were initially in standard Grey-Green livery. However, the acquisition of the Kentish Town-based coaching division of the very old established Birch Bros., fleet, in February 1971, prompted certain coaches to receive Birch fleetnames, as seen on WLT 579G in July 1972, a practice discontinued in 1977.

G. R. Mills

HERE'S TO YOU MESSRS ROBINSONS!

Plate 211: The LHL found early favour with the well-known and old established W. Robinson & Sons (Tours) Ltd., of Gt. Harwood, Lancs., as three were delivered in April 1969. The following year, a pair of both LHL and LH joined the fleet. One of the former is seen here at Haverhill, Suffolk, a pioneer new town, bound for Clacton-on-Sea in July 1975. The high gloss paintwork is typical of the distinct green and black coaches operated, but frequently-sold vehicles from the fleet are not repainted in the new owner's colours. In fact, two East Anglian operators adopted Robinson's livery as their own!

G. R. Mills

Plate 212: In the early spring of each year, from 1971-73, four LH breed/ Plaxton coaches were delivered to Robinson's which, with the seven already in stock, occupied fleet numbers 151-169 inclusive. Both the 1971 and 1972 orders were for three LH with 45 seat and one LHL with a 51 seat body. One of the former was purchased by Thomas Bros., of Llangadog, Dyfed, in 1976 and is seen here against the ruins of Llandovery's Norman Castle in June 1980. The Welsh owners have repainted the coach into their own cream and green livery, with red lettering.

G. R. Mills

Plate 213: Of the eighteen new to Robinson's, eight were purchased by Bassett's Coachways Ltd. of Tittensor, Staffs. All were repainted in their distinctive RAF blue livery, embellished with their metal-winged motif which is removed when the coach is sold. NWW 162K, seen arriving at Wembley Stadium in March 1981 with a load of schoolgirls for the annual international hockey match, was the only LHL vehicle in the 1972 intake. Bassett's have been highly successful contestants in both the coach rallies at Blackpool and Wolverhampton for several years, originally using the LHL coaches and, later, Leyland products.

G. R. Mills

LHs in Tandem

Plate 214: Bishop Auckland market place, in November 1983, sees two ex-London Transport LHs employed on local services by the renowned OK Motor Services. Smartly repainted in duo red and cream, they stand where once their former London double deckers stood (in recent times DMS, and RTL class some years earlier).

M. Fowler

Plate 215: Two LH6L vehicles with Plaxton Elite 45 seater bodies of different pedigrees. KPM 429P, on the left, was new to Blue Saloon Coaches of Guildford in November 1975. The example on the right was new in September 1975 to Sheenway Coaches of London SW14, whose fleet of five in 1977 was all LH. KVD 449P was acquired by King's Coaches of Stanway, near Colchester, in February 1979, and was seen in April 1983 en route to Cobham with PSV Circle members from Colchester.

G. R. Mills

Plate 216: Seen at the regular coach-gathering high spot on Dartmoor, these two Devon General LHs have stopped to allow their tourist passengers time to view the famous prison at Princetown, and the bleak surrounding countryside. JFJ 504/5N have the special narrow Plaxton coachwork and have received the frontal grille modification, to allow extra air circulation, as can be clearly seen in this September 1982 view.

D. G. Savage

LITTLE 'UNS HUNT IN PAIRS

Plate 217: A new operator, formed late in 1983 in Hertfordshire, emerged as Regis Coaches Ltd., of Bishops Stortford. The company title is cunningly derived from the proprietor's christian name, (i.e. Reg's coaches!). To continue the regal association the adopted livery is a royal purple with gold lining. Both Plaxton Supreme bodies were new in 1978. TCE 131S (left) was a former Miller Bros., Foxton, Cambs., coach, whilst BKJ 462T was ex-Supreme, Hadleigh, Essex, although new to Pilchers, Chatham.

G. R. Mills

Plate 218: Famed for Daimler CVD double deckers of longevity, it is less well-known that five LHS models were purchased by the long-established Gash of Newark, Notts. One was a standard Plaxton coach, and the remaining four received Marshall bodies. Two of each style were specified, i.e. a 1973 bus (first LHS supplied to an independent) with an indentical vehicle in 1975 (left), whilst a pair of dual-purpose versions were delivered, one in 1975 (right) and the other, finally, in 1980. Numbered BR1-5, all were attired in duo green and cream, as per the illustrated pair seen at Newark in July 1983.

G. R. Mills

Plate 219: Epsom Coaches, operated by H. R. Richmond Ltd., have purchased the largest number of privately-owned examples of the LHS model, all bought new. The first arrived in 1975, and by 1982 eleven had been taken into stock. Two examples are seen on the forecourt of the firm's modern premises in August 1980. KGT 895N (left), new in July 1975, was sold to Camden Coaches of Sevenoaks, Kent, in December 1981. RGF 230P stayed in Surrey a year longer before being purchased by Goodwins of Black Notley, near Braintree, Essex. Repainted silver-grey and blue, it gained a class award at the Showbus Rally at Woburn Abbey in September 1983, when on hire to Colchester members of the PSV Circle.

G. R. Mills

THE FIRST AND LAST **LHL**

Plate 220: Whilst the bulk of the LH production was supplied to the National Bus, ex-Tilling companies, all the LHL chassis were built for the private sector. The initial production batch included three for F. G. Wilder, t/a Golden Miller of Feltham, which were delivered in June 1968. TMT 763F, which carried chassis No. 101, is seen at the Duke of Wellington refreshment halt, at Hatfield Peverel on the A12 trunk road, in August 1970.

G. R. Mills

Plate 221: The final LHL coach chassis built was supplied to Kettlewell's of Retford, Notts., in April 1979. It joined a mixed fleet of AEC Bedford, Ford and Leyland coaches, at least one of each chassis make having been supplied new. The Plaxton Supreme 53 seater was delivered in the distinctive fleet livery of white and black, with gold stripes. The vehicle was seen on the outskirts of its home town, in July 1979, during a test drive gratefully granted to the photographer.

G. R. Mills

PAIRS OF BIG BRISTOLS

Plate 222: Only four LHL chassis were bodied by Duples. Two were supplied to regular LH breed customer, F. G. Wilder, t/a 'Golden Miller', Feltham, in August 1983. The second pair went into service with Wilde, t/a Mitcham Belle, of Mitcham, Surrey, in May 1975. JGP 237/8N, the latter duo are seen at Blackpool, prior to delivery.

G. R. Mills Collection

Plate 223: In the shade of a huge horse-chestnut tree, two LHLs stand side by side at Colchester bus station in May 1981. GME 981J (left) was one of a trio new to 'Golden Miller', Feltham, in 1971, and had three owners before purchase by Victoria Coaches, Rochford, near Southend, as shown. Alongside is WVB 265G, a 1969 example which was kept in immaculate condition whilst operated by Mann, Island Travel of Canvey. In September 1981 this Plaxton Elite-bodied coach was exported to Jamaica by Arlington Motors, Potters Bar.

G. R. Mills

Plate 224: In 1969, the largest single order for LHL chassis was placed with Kirkby, South Anston, by Margo's Europa Coaches of London SE19. In the event, only six were delivered and the balance, all consecutively registered, was diverted to other customers. DWT 637H (right) was one of the initial sextet passed via Poulson, t/a Roadliner, South Benfleet, Essex, to Shirley, t/a Pams, Enderby, Leics. It meets DWT 642H, one of the later diverts, which had five previous owners, two of which were Scottish, prior to being with Partridge & Son, Hadleigh, Suffolk. The vehicles are seen together at Colchester's Searchlight Tattoo in August 1982.

G. R. Mills

REREGISTERED REBUILT REBODIED

Plate 225: The first day out for the Eagle Coaches of Bristol LHS as 110 LYB was 17th March 1984, and it is seen arriving at the Wembley Stadium complex. Currently attired in white, with orange and lemon stripes, the coach was previously in a mundane red and cream, which was the 'Eagle' livery when the LHS was acquired in November 1976. It was previously owned by the well-known rally award winning firm of G. K. Kinch of Mountsorrell, Leics., with whom it was then registered JLE 44N, having been new in May 1975.

G. R. Mills

Plate 226: New in Hull, and now on its third owner, but still in the Hull area, GRH 321L was supplied to Going Places (International) Ltd., t/a Halcyon Tours, in May 1973. It passed to Nippy Coaches, Sutton-on-Hull, in April 1977. The addresses of the operators are noteworthy, i.e. Halcyon was Land of Green Ginger whilst Nippy was Garden Village! Seen at Gt. Yarmouth in August 1983 with its third owner, Phil Danby Coaches of Burton Pidsea, the LHL is one of very few Elite-bodied models to receive a Supreme style updated frontal rebuild.

G. R. Mills

Plate 227: The first private operator to place a multiple order for LHS chassis coaches was H. R. Richmond Ltd., who operate the immaculate Epsom Coaches from the Surrey town of the same name. The first three were delivered in April 1975 as GNM 232-4N. The latest of these met with an unfortunate accident, during 1976, which wrecked the body. The chassis was rejuvenated and returned to Plaxtons at Scarborough for a new Supreme body, as original, but without the traditional Bristol dome. In January 1977 it re-entered the fleet as UGC 229R and is seen in August 1980 outside the company's first-class premises.

G. R. Mills

WesterBUS

Plate 228: The most northerly-based LHS is undoubtedly WST 79V, owned by M. E. Taylor of Badbea in Wester Ross, who trades as Westerbus. The ECW body, supplied new in November 1979, has 27 coach seats and a carpetted floor. The white and navy blue vehicle works the 80 mile summer service from Gairloch to Inverness, a 3½ hour journey - a tribute to LH stamina! The driver has stopped for a well-earned 'cuppa' at this Muir of Ord café, in this September 1983 view.

S. J. Brown

InterBUS

Plate 229: Western National's discontinuation of various services in the Dorchester area of Dorset prompted Barry's Coaches Ltd., of Weymouth, to venture into stage operation, adopting the fleetname 'Interbus', as shown on VMO 233H, an ex-Thames Valley LH/ECW in the white and golden brown livery used on all the bus fleet. The vehicle is at Wool railway station, having worked the weekday service from Lulworth Cove in June 1983.

A. J. Kennedy

Hampshire BUS

Plate 230: Both Eastern National and Hants & Dorset reserved their 9000 class for the non-PSV ancillary vehicles. The Chief Engineer, having held posts with both companies, is the common factor. No. 9078 (NLJ 526M) is seen at Southampton, in October 1983, in its new role as an engineering towing wagon. A twin, NLJ 528M is similarly converted as No. 9087 and is based at Poole depot, now a Wilts & Dorset works.

D. G. Savage

IRISH INTERLUDE

Plates 231 & 232: Only four LHL chassis were fitted with Plaxton Panorama I coach bodies. Three were supplied to F. G. Wilder, t/a 'Golden Miller', Feltham, whilst the fourth went across the sea to Ireland. Supplied to PAB Transport of Dublin, an Irish company formed by Sealandair of West Bromwich in 1950, BZO 840 was delivered in 1968. Seen *(above)* back on the mainland in August 1975, the duo green and grey coach was caught in bright sunshine on the seafront at Llandudno, whilst the distant clouds threaten some heavy rain! The year 1969 saw a rash of orders for the new Plaxton Elite body, with Grey-Green, London; Mayne, Manchester and Robinson, Gt. Harwood each buying a trio on the LHL chassis. Similarly PAB Transport purchased a pair, one of which, GZU 613, is seen in Aldgate, London, in April 1979. Both coaches were later owned by M. Byrne, Kilcock Coaches, Co. Kildare.

G. R. Mills

THE LH . . . A BUS FOR ALL REASONS

MAJORETTE BAND

Plate 233: MUO 338F was the last of the initial batch of fifteen LH/ECW buses supplied to Western National in 1968. Traded in to Ensign, dealer, of Purfleet, when ex-London DMS double deckers were supplied in 1980/1, the displaced saloons found a variety of new owners. The example was repainted black with an orange-red window surround/bumper and door frames, for a troupe of young lasses, as shown here at Ensign bus yard in October 1981.

G. R. Mills

SHIPPING LINE

Plate 234: POD 813H was one of the third batch of twenty two supplied to Western National. ECW had redesigned the front panel with the introduction of a ribbed (strengthened) section of the fibreglass panel around the headlights, and repositioned the foglamps. It has been superbly repainted into an ivory and pale blue livery, for transfers out of Harwich and Parkeston quays, for DFDS Seaways/Prins Ferries by Hook's of Gt. Oakley; a company then owned by Staines Crusader, of Clacton-on-Sea. The smart bus is seen in Colchester bus station waiting to load local bus enthusiasts for their annual pilgrimage to the Southend Bus Rally in June 1982.

G. R. Mills

EDUCATIONAL ESTABLISHMENT

Plate 235: A view of the earliest curved windsceen style ECW body. Later the front light clusters were restyled (see examples on introduction pages). XEL 826K was the second of a batch of sixteen supplied jointly to both Hants & Dorset (10), and Wilts & Dorset (6). As with the Western National LHs, this example was dispatched to Ensign, bus dealers, at Purfleet, when the DMS invaded the southern counties. This October 1983 view shows the vehicle repainted white and red for a local school. In the background *(right)* is a preserved Green Line RT, and *(left)* an ex-Western SMT Lodekka.

G. R. Mills

BRISTOL LH/LHS* SUPPLIED TO MAJOR OPERATORS

NATIONAL BUS COMPANY

Fleet No.	Registration No.	Body Builder	Type & Capacity	Year New
Alder Valley				
535-41	KPA 346-52P	ECW	B43F	1975
Bristol				
351-6	DHW 291-6K	ECW	B43F	1971/2
357-64	JHW 117-124P	ECW	B43F	1975
365-82	KHU 315-30, 615/6P	ECW	B43F	1976
383-6	JOU 162-5P	ECW	B43F	1976
387-9	KHY 430-2P	ECW	B43F	1976
390-5	OFB 963-8R	ECW	B43F	1977
396-400	OTC 604-8R	ECW	B43F	1977
401-21	REU 312-32S	ECW	B43F	1977
422-8	SWS 768-74S	ECW	B43F	1978
429-33	TTC 786-90T	ECW	B43F	1978
434-53	WAE 186-93, 294/5T	ECW	B43F	1979
454-66	AFB 585-97V	ECW	B43F	1980
Crosville				
SLP 144-8	CFM 144-8G	ECW	B45F	1969
SLP 149-59	DFM 149-59H	ECW	B45F	1969/70
SLL 601-6	KMA 531-6N	ECW	B43F	1975
SLL 607-10	LMA 607-10P	ECW	B43F	1975
SLL 611-20	MCA 611-20P	ECW	B43F	1975
SLL 621-40	OCA 621-40P	ECW	B43F	1976
Cumberland				
100/1	WAO 100-1H	ECW	B45F	1970
1310	WAO 289H	Plaxton	C45F	1970
102-5	XAO 732-5H	ECW	B45F	1970
106-16	XRM 106-116J	ECW	B45F	1970
East Kent				
1559-62*	GFN 559-62N	ECW	B35F	1975
East Midland				
523-32	UNN 523-32G	Willowbrook	B45F	1969
851-3	SNU 851-3R	ECW	B43F	1977
854-7	WVO 854-7S	ECW	B43F	1978
Eastern Counties				
LH685-92	RAH 685-92F	ECW	B45F	1968
LH693-5	UNG 693-5G	ECW	B45F	1969
LH696-702	VAH 696-702H	ECW	B45F	1969
LHS 595-9	WNG 101-5H	ECW	B37F	1970
LH899-901	WNG 899-901H	ECW	B45F	1970
LH902-6	XPW 902-6H	ECW	B45F	1970
LH907-11	YAH 907-11H	ECW	B45F	1970
LH912-6	YPW 912-6H	ECW	B45F	1970
LH523-6	CNG 523-6K	ECW	B45F	1971
LH527-31	DNG 527-31K	ECW	B45F	1971/2
LH532	DPW 532K	ECW	B45F	1972
LH533/4	FNG 533/4K	ECW	B45F	1972
LH535/6	GNG 535/6K	ECW	B45F	1972
LH537	HAH 537L	ECW	B45F	1972
LH923/17-22	TCL 136-42R	ECW	B43F	1977
LH924-31	WEX 924-31S	ECW	B43F	1977/8
Eastern National				
1100-3	UVX 4-7S	ECW	B43F	1977
Greenslades				
317-28	JFJ 497-508N	Plaxton	C45F	1975
Hants & Dorset				
828	NLJ 817G	ECW	B39D	1968
3026-8	REL 743-5H	ECW	B39D	1969
3029-35	RLJ 789-95H	ECW	B39D	1969/70
3051-5	TRU 220-4J	ECW	B39D	1970
3056/7	ULJ 367/8J	ECW	B43F	1970
1539-48	XEL 825-34K	ECW	B43F	1971/2
3501-10	DEL 537-46L	ECW	B43F	1973
3511-4	NEL 844-7M	ECW	B43F	1973
3515-29	NLJ 515-29M	ECW	B43F	1973/4
3530-41	ORU 530-41M	ECW	B43F	1974
3542-61	GLJ 474-93N	ECW	B43F	1974/5
3562-76	HJT 34-48N	ECW	B43F	1975
3577-9	HPR 395-7N	ECW	B43F	1975
3806-11	LJT 939-44P	ECW	B43F	1975

NATIONAL BUS COMPANY

Fleet No.	Registration No.	Body Builder	Type & Capacity	Year New
Lincolnshire				
1651-6	GVL 907-12F	ECW	DP41F	1968
1801-3*	GVL 913-5G	ECW	B35F	1968/9
1804*	JVL 701G	ECW	B35F	1969
1805-10*	JVL 616-8, 927-9H	ECW	B35F	1969
1657-61	JVL 363/4, 613-5G	ECW	DP41F	1969
1001-6	KFE 296-9, 301/2H	ECW	B43F	1969/70
1007-10	LVL 371/2, 901/2J	ECW	B43F	1970
1662	JVL 926H	ECW	DP41F	1970
1663-8	KVL 449-54H	ECW	DP41F	1970
1669-74	NFE 644-9J	ECW	DP41F	1971
1011-4	NVL 448-50, 613K	ECW	B43F	1971
1015-8	OVL 448/9/51/2K	ECW	B43F	1972
1019	RFE 432K	ECW	B43F	1972
1020-2	RVL 248/9/51L	ECW	B43F	1972
1023-6	SVL 20-3L	ECW	B43F	1973
1027-9	UVL 572-4M	ECW	B43F	1973
1030-5	WFE 675-9, 839M	ECW	B43F	1974
1036-40	JTL 774-8M	ECW	B43F	1975
1041-4	LTL 660-3P	ECW	B43F	1975
1045-52	SVL 830-7R	ECW	B43F	1977
1053-7	UFE 286-90R	ECW	B43F	1977
1054-61	XFW 949-56S	ECW	B43F	1977/8
1062-3	YVL 836-7S	ECW	B43F	1978
1064-72	DTL 540-8T	ECW	B43F	1978/9
London Country				
BL1-11*	RPH 101-111L	ECW	B35F	1973
BL12-23*	SPK 112-123L	ECW	B35F	1973
BL24-30*	XPD 124-130N	ECW	B35F	1974
BL31-53*	GPD 299-321N	ECW	B35F	1974
BN 54-67*	TPJ 54-67S	ECW	B35F	1977
Mansfield District				
107-110	BNU 669-72G	ECW	B45F	1969
Midland General				
111-6	BNU 673-8G	ECW	B45F	1969
117-21	JRB 768-77J	ECW	B45F	1970
122-4	ORB 248-50K	ECW	B45F	1971
National Welsh				
MD8023-8*	GTX 758-63W	ECW	DP27F	1980
MD8114-6*	KWO 568-70X	ECW	DP27F	1981
Ribble				
271/2*	FBV 271/2W	ECW	B35F	1980
Southern Vectis				
825/6	LDL 262/3F	ECW	B43F	1968
832-5*	NDL 768-771G	ECW	B35F	1969
827-9	PDL 489-91H	ECW	B43F	1970
836-9*	HDL 412-5N	ECW	B35F	1975
DP2-4*	KDL 202-4W	ECW	DP31F	1980
Thames Valley				
C428-31	RJB 428-31F	Duple	C41F	1968
C432-5	UMO 688-91G	Duple	C41F	1969
257-64	RRX 991-8G	ECW	B45F	1969
265-8	VMO 225-8H	ECW	B45F	1969
273/4	XRX 819/20H	ECW	B45F	1970
C436-9	YBL 925-8H	Duple	C41F	1970
275/6	ABL 121/2J	ECW	B45F	1970
277-80	AMO 235-8J	ECW	B45F	1970
Timpsons				
*	THX 618M	ECW	DP29F	1973
Trent				
388/9*	PNU 388/9R	ECW	B35F	1976
384-7	SNU 384-7R	ECW	B43F	1977
390/1	STO 390/1R	ECW	B43F	1977

NATIONAL BUS COMPANY

Fleet No.	Registration No.	Body Builder	Type & Capacity	Year New
United				
LH1-5	THN 601-5F	ECW	B45F	1968
LH6/8/10	UHN 796/8/800G	ECW	B45F	1968
LH7/9	THN 607/9F	ECW	B45F	1968
1511-4	YHN 811-4H	ECW	B45F	1968
1515-20	AHN 315-20H	ECW	B45F	1969/70
1081-5	BHN 981-5H	Plaxton	C41F	1970
1521-54	PHN 521-54L	ECW	B43F	1972/3
1555-70	VHN 855-70M	ECW	B43F	1973
1571-1600	WHN 571-600M	ECW	B43F	1973/4
1601-12	AHN 601-12M	ECW	B43F	1974
1613-34	GUP 897-918N	ECW	B43F	1974/5
1635-45	HUP 791-801N	ECW	B43F	1975
1646-55	LGR 646-55P	ECW	B43F	1975
1656-61	MGR 656-61P	ECW	B43F	1975
1662-5	NBR 662-5P	ECW	B43F	1975
1666-85	NGR 666-85P	ECW	B43F	1976
1686-9	XPT 686-9R	ECW	B43F	1977
1690-3	XUP 690-3R	ECW	B43F	1977
1694-700	CGR 894-900S	ECW	B43F	1977/8
1701-11	LPT 701-11T	ECW	B43F	1979
1712-4	MUP 712-4T	ECW	B43F	1979
1715-8	SUP 715-8V	ECW	B43F	1979
United Counties				
400/1	SRP 400/1G	ECW	B45F	1969
402/3	TBD 402/3G	ECW	B45F	1969
404-12	XBD 404-12J	ECW	B45F	1970
Western National/Devon General				
712-26	MUO 324-38F	ECW	B41F	1968
727-9/32-4	PTA 757-62G	ECW	B43F	1969
730/1/5-40/50-63	POD 801-22H	ECW	B43F	1969/70
1300-11	RDV 435-46H	Duple	C41F	1970
1564-7	SUO 429-32H	ECW	B43F	1970
1568-70	TTA 557-8, 737H	ECW	B43F	1970
1571-4	TUO 265-8J	ECW	B43F	1970/1
1312-5	UTT 578-81J	Plaxton	C41F	1971
88-93*	VOD 88-93K	Marshall	B33F	1971
1575-88	VOD 106-19K	ECW	B43F	1971/2
1250-5*	VOD 120-5K	Marshall	B33F	1972
1316/8	BDV 316/8L	Marshall	C39F	1973
1589-1600	NFJ 589-600M	ECW	B43F	1973
1317/9-25	NTT 317/9-25M	Marshall	C39F	1973
1601-6	PTT 601-6M	ECW	B43F	1974
100-3	PUO 100-3M	ECW	B43F	1974
1326-31	PUO 326-31M	ECW	B43F	1974
1607-11; 104-7	GDV 456-64N	ECW	B43F	1974/5
1612-21	HTT 367-76N	ECW	B43F	1975
1622;108-115; 1623	KTT 37-46P	ECW	B43F	1975
3100-3, 3400-7	PTT 70-3, 100-7R	Plaxton	C41F	1977
3408-13, 3114-23, 3104-23	SFJ 108-33R	Plaxton	C41F	1977
116-21	STT 408-13R	ECW	B43F	1977
1624-30	VDV 124-30S	ECW	B43F	1977/8
3124-6	VDV 131-3S	Plaxton	C41F	1978
3127-9	VOD 627-9S	Plaxton	C41F	1978
3130-4	AFJ 691-5T	Plaxton	C41F	1978
3300-23	AFJ 720-43T	Plaxton	C41F	1979
1561-3*	FDV 791-3V	ECW	B35F	1979
94-6*	LFJ 848-50W	ECW	B35F	1980
Western Welsh				
1	MB0 1F	Weymann	B30F	1968
West Yorkshire				
LH1/3/8/2	YWT 164-6, 700G	ECW	B45F	1969
LH4/5	YWU 981/2G	ECW	B45F	1969
LH6/7	YWW 540/1G	ECW	B45F	1969
KLH9/10	YWX 221/2G	ECW	B45F	1969
LH11	YYG 786G	ECW	B45F	1969
LH12-19	AWR 338-40,883-7G	ECW	B45F	1969
LH20	AWY 239G	ECW	B45F	1969
LH21	AWT 614G	ECW	B45F	1969
LH22	BWU 554H	ECW	B45F	1969
LH23	BWW 154H	ECW	B45F	1969
LH24	BYG 135H	ECW	B45F	1969
LH25/6	CWR 273-4H	ECW	B45F	1969
1177-82	OWT 783-8M	ECW	B45F	1973/4
Wilts & Dorset				
521-3	REL 746-8H	ECW	B39D	1969
524-6	RRU 692-4H	ECW	B39D	1969
527/8	TRU 227/8J	ECW	B39D	1970
529/30	UEL 567/8J	ECW	B43F	1970

SCOTTISH BUS GROUP

Fleet No.	Registration No.	Body Builder	Type & Capacity	Year New
Alexander Midland				
MLH1-8	SMS 671-8H	Alexander	C38F	1970
MLH9-19	SWG 669-79H	Alexander	C38F	1970
MLH20-5	WMS 920-5J	Alexander	C41F	1971
MLH26-33	WWG 326-33J	Alexander	C41F	1971
MLH34-8	BWG 334-8L	Alexander	C41F	1972
MLH39-41	BWG 339-41L	Alexander	B45F	1972
Scottish Omnibus (Eastern Scottish)				
YA315-32	OSF 315-32G	Alexander	C38F	1970
YA333-48	SFS 333-48H	Alexander	C38F	1970

TRANSPORT EXECUTIVES/MUNICIPALITIES

Fleet No.	Registration No.	Body Builder	Type & Capacity	Year New
Cardiff				
104/5*	LUH 104/5P	ECW	DP27F	1976
Greater Glasgow PTE				
C1*	VDS 216R	Plaxton	C35F	1977
Greater Manchester PTE/Lancashire United				
318-37	UTD 281-300H	Northern Counties	B39D	1969/70
1320-5	BNE 763-8N	ECW	B43F	1974
92/3*	JND 992/3N	Duple	C29F	1925
98*	PNE 360R	Duple	C29F	1976
London Transport				
BS1-6*	GHV 501-6N	ECW	B26F	1975
BL1-40	KJD 401-40P	ECW	B39F	1976
BS7-17*	OJD 7-17R	ECW	B26F	1976/7
BL41-95	OJD 41-95R	ECW	B39F	1976/7
Northampton				
21/2*	KBD 21/2V	ECW	DP30F	1979
Preston				
342-4*	PHG 242-4P	Duple	DP31F	1976
Rossendale				
50-1*	SND 550/1X	East Lancs	B28F	1982
West Yorks PTE				
36-41*	JUG 352-7N	ECW	B27F	1975
42-7*	MUA 42-7P	ECW	B27F	1976

POSTSCRIPT AN EXAMPLE OF A VERY NON-PSV LHL

Plate 236: Lawrence Wilson & Sons Ltd., of Guisley, Yorkshire, manufacturers of well-known one/or twin small person carriages (i.e. Silver Cross Prams) have had eleven LHL and three LH chassis fitted with pantechnicon bodies, from new, from 1972-7. The example below is a smart 1975 vehicle with a Van Plan body, of Warrington, and is seen at Penarth, near Cardiff, in July 1981.

G. R. Mills